Informal Markets in Developing Countries

Informal Markets in Developing Countries

N. Vijay Jagannathan

New York   Oxford
Oxford University Press, Inc.
1987

Oxford University Press

Oxford   New York   Toronto
Delhi   Bombay   Calcútta   Madras   Karachi
Petaling Jaya   Singapore   Hong Kong   Tokyo
Nairobi   Dar es Salaam   Cape Town
Melbourne   Auckland

and associated companies in
Beirut   Berlin   Ibadan   Nicosia

Library of Congress Cataloging-in-Publication Data
Jagannathan, N. Vijay.
Informal markets in developing countries.
Bibliography: p.   Includes index.
1. Informal sector (Economics)—Developing countries. I. Title.
HD2346.5.J34   1986   381   86–2345
ISBN 0–19–504088–0

9 8 7 6 5 4 3 2 1

Printed in the United States of America
on acid-free paper

This book is dedicated
to the memory of my father, R. L. Narasimham
of the Indian Civil Service,
former Chief Justice of
Patna and Orissa high courts.
His erudition inspired me to explore
some uncharted areas of economics.

Preface

The poor, like the affluent, have to make hard economic decisions, except that their decisions are made in informal markets where formal legal norms rarely penetrate. On a hot, dusty day, in one of the villages of West Bengal, I met a villager who seemed to epitomize the kind of people who spend their lives in informal markets. The Family Planning campaign was in full swing that day and we picked a farmer at random to ask his views on the subject.

The farmer began his answer by saying, "Sir, I am an illiterate farmer. Whenever I plow my land I find that despite my best effort the furrow created by my plow is never a straight line. In the same way I, think my speech today is likely to veer off the subject because I lack education. Please excuse me for this lapse." Dressed in the shabbiest of clothes, and looking much older than his age, the farmer was clearly one of the faceless poor about whom so much has been written and analyzed. Perhaps he was more poetic than the others we spoke to, but the anecdote indicates that, like them—in terms of rationality and common sense—there was nothing ignorant about him.

The farmer and millions of others like him make their economic decisions in informal markets marked by highly personalized relations between transactors. The rules of business in production and exchange get shaped by informal institutional arrangements that have not so far been adequately conceptualized by social scientists. This book seeks to explain, in the traditions of positive economics, how informal contracts are put to productive and unproductive use by the poor and the wealthy in developing countries. Several policy issues emerge, which will be of interest to any person interested in economic development.

Thirteen years of observation and research have gone into the writing of this book. The observations were made during the years I have spent as an official in the Indian Administrative Service in the villages, towns, and cities of West Bengal. The opportunity to distill the thoughts arose when I was awarded a fellowship for doctoral studies in economics at Boston University.

Dr. Michael Manove was the single most important mentor who made a set of vague ideas take concrete shape. Without his help this work would perhaps never have begun. Dr. David Wheeler was another great source of help and encouragement. I am grateful to both of them for the time and attention given to me.

I would also like to thank Dr. V. S. Vyas for his valuable insights into the structure of rural markets. Professors Gustav Papanek and Paul Streeten devoted considerable time to encouraging me to develop these ideas.

My debt of gratitude also extends to Dr. Ashok Mitra, former Finance Minister of West Bengal and Mr. P. K. Sarkar, Secretary Finance Department, Government of West Bengal for having been gracious enough to permit me a long leave of absence to revise the manuscript for the book. I would also like to thank Mr. Herbert J. Addison of Oxford University Press and an anonymous referee for making this publication possible.

Last but not least, my thanks to my dear wife Sheila, whose unpaid labor was as great as mine, and my son Jayant, who—at least until now—has been my most consistent admirer.

Contents

Informal Markets in Developing Countries

1

The Logic of Unorganized Markets

"What is a cynic? A man who knows the price
of everything, and the value of nothing."

This remark by Oscar Wilde could be adapted to highlight the fact
that during market exchange of goods and services, economists have
tended to ignore the value of interpersonal and social relationships.
Such invisible but valuable behavioral assets actually exist in all economic systems, but they acquire particular significance during the
process of economic development. An understanding of these relations will enable the reader to appreciate the logic of market relations
in unorganized markets of developing countries.

Markets in these countries do not fit the smoothly operating institutions assumed by standard neoclassical economics. Information
among transactors in both factor and product markets is usually scarce
and often incomplete because many Western-style institutions are
either partially developed or underdeveloped. Various implicit or informal contracts through personalized interchanges become methods of circumventing the problem of imperfect information during
production or exchange.[1] These contracts enable individuals to generate and appropriate different amounts of economic rent.

The roots of these issues can be traced to inadequacies in the legal
and administrative system. Laws and rules are often unable to monitor and police economic transactions and assure equality of access
to everyone. Insurance against risks is at best partial, if not restricted
to a privileged few. For a vast majority of transactors in the market
economy, therefore, regular behavioral relations become necessary
methods of defining the "rules of business." As long as these relational contracts are stable over periods of time, they can be expected
to generate private and often social wealth.

One obviously has to guard against generalizations. Even in the poorest of developing countries there are some markets, in what can be described as the *organized* sector, which function within the framework of civil laws and administrative regulations. This sector comprises joint stock companies, public sector enterprises, multinational companies, large proprietary concerns, and commercial plantations to name a few, and is virtually indistinguishable from its Western counterpart. In fact, as the origins are often traceable to a colonial period (usually English or French), the traditions of law and economics, organizational theory, and business management can be easily adapted and applied to understand their workings.

Outside the pale of the organized sector is the *unorganized* or *informal* sector, covering economic transactions of anywhere between 30 percent and 70 percent of the countries' gross national products. It covers most rural markets, and the peripheral but growing urban informal sector. Very often appearing to be chaotic, sometimes complex, and occasionally intriguing, this sector has the markets where the poor earn their livelihood.

The unorganized sector is at best a loose way to describe a wide range of economic activities by small firms, households, and individuals, which are to varying degrees integrated with organized sector markets. At one end of the spectrum a family firm, for example, may be closely integrated with a large corporation in the organized sector through industrial subcontracting. At the other end, agricultural laborers and slum or shantytown dwellers could be securing their income-earning opportunities solely within the unorganized sector.

Such individuals and institutions straddle a nether world between tradition and change: social and cultural groupings such as castes, tribes, and clans continue to play significant roles in their daily lives, but at the same time pressures of modernization and change impinge directly on their economic decision-making process. With the monetization of the economy, rights and privileges of status-based relations have been disrupted, and often destroyed. The affected poor could not affort to sit and watch the world go by; instead they have had to identify every economic opportunity available and seek to earn income from them all. In these situations, newly emerging earning opportunities or economic entitlements are protected by implicit contracts in unorganized markets.

The critical test of a transition from an insular, subsistence type of life to productive activities in unorganized markets comes about when perceived economic opportunities are seized upon and utilized by negotiating and executing contracts that are stable over a period of time. The contracting processes involve the execution of voluntary agreements, which define rights and obligations of individuals in specific business transactions, instead of involuntary agreements based on status, as in a primitive subsistence-oriented community.[2]

If these contracts are honored over a reasonable length of time, they could serve as effective substitutes for many institutional deficiencies. Take, for example, a landowner in an overpopulated country like India or Bangladesh. Although labor may be available in abundance, a hirer still faces problems in securing a supply of "reliable" and "trustworthy" workers who can be depended upon to render services during emergencies both on the farm and at the home of the hirer.[3] Workers who are willing to make required behavioral adjustments could then be paid wages above their marginal product as *tied rents*. In other situations, behavioral contracts can be used to restrict universal access to earning opportunities, allowing participants to earn rents in the process.

There are several examples of individuals and groups utilizing behavioral relations to acquire access to earning opportunities. Ethnic and tribal groups in Asia and Africa sometimes utilized traditional social norms to execute complex business contracts. For instance, in Ghana, early in this century, some individuals perceived economic opportunities in cocoa cultivation without having the suitable land.[4] Other tribal groups controlled access to such lands "owned" as communal property. There were no institutions that could facilitate a market transaction between the two groups. Two responses emerged. Some of these entrepreneurs utilized their existing kin relations to negotiate collectively for land. Others, who did not have extended family connections, informally contracted with strangers to form "companies," and again collectively negotiated for lands. The resultant group solidarity in both cases was vital so that negotiations could be conducted (a) from a position of equality with the landowning tribal groups, and (b) to ensure that the latter did not renege the land deals.

Once the groups secured land rights, individual members invested in their cocoa farms independently, and operated their private farms with full autonomy. These associations served as effective proxies for the formal legal system, and thus resulted in effective use of behavioral relations to generate wealth.

The theme of this book is that in unorganized markets of developing countries several analogous income-earning opportunities exist that are recognized and exploited through implicit contracts. Individuals are able to earn varying amounts of income, often in the form of economic rents, by segmenting markets and restricting universal access. The importance of these arrangements is that they are the means by which many of the poor are able to earn income larger than that predicted by standard economic theory.[5] Access to such rents will obviously be highly unequal, implying that among all sections of society opportunities for economic advancement depend critically on the rent-earning opportunities a person is entitled to.[6]

To sum up, behavioral relations are viewed at two levels. At a primary level, regularity in these relations over time ensures for participants a set of economic entitlements or economic rights by assuring them access to income streams. These rights are extralegal in the sense that they are neither sanctioned nor protected by the legal system and are usually nontradable, although for the concerned recipients they are valued economic rights. At a secondary level, such arrangements outline the contours of a set of informal institutions, whose boundaries determine the nature and scope of access to income for members of the work force in unorganized markets. While the primary level is concerned with the forms and substance of informal contracts, the secondary level deals primarily with the institutional consequences of these relations.

Behavioral Relations in Economic Literature

Before concluding this chapter, it will be useful to discuss briefly how behavioral relations have been viewed by some of the other institutional literature. Most of the literature, having been influenced by the Western experience, views behavioral relations within a given framework of laws, property relations, and formal business organizations.

Consider first the Marxian framework. The behavioral relations are defined by existing (tangible) property relations, pattern of ownership, and division of labor (all collectively constituting relations of production), as well as by the productive forces. Marx describes how these forces, under capitalism, reduce social relations to an impersonal cash nexus.[7] A fairly clear inference is that the Marxian analysis has elaborated a theory of the *consequences* of impersonal behavioral relations in market systems. The ironclad guarantees given by the Western "rule of law" are assumed to operate efficiently.

In an analogous manner, literature on industrial organization has analyzed behavioral relations within business firms and corporations. Alchian and Demsetz, for instance, describe how the importance of teamwork has led to the evolution of institutional designs that ensure efficient monitoring of each team member's performance.[8] Lieben-stein, in contrast, has taken a more pessimistic line, and explains through the X-efficiency hypothesis the way in which individuals in large organizations utilize varying degrees of effort levels during their workday.[9] Recent literature has also examined behavioral opportun-ism in appropriating quasi-rents, leading to the vertical integration of firms. The behavioral and organizational consequences of the principal-agent distinction have also been developed extensively.[10] Finally, the theory of rent seeking describes the consequences of public policy restrictions such as import quotas on behavioral relations. In-dividuals are hypothesized to respond to these opportunities by spending valuable resources in lobbying and other rent-seeking strat-egies in order to capture the artificially created transfers arising out of public policy.[11] In all these writings, behavioral relations have been analyzed as a consequence of existing institutions, laws, or adminis-trative rules.

Some recent literature has attempted to break away from the es-tablished mold. In a stimulating article, Yoram Ben Porath has ex-plored the range of uses to which informal social networks are put during economic activities.[12] Recently, Robert Pollak has extended the traditions of institutional economics to explain the importance of families in economic relationships.[13] In the developing country con-text, Binswanger and Rosenzweig have explored how behavioral re-lations are utilized to reduce risks and to insure against hunger.[14] Binswanger and Rosenzweig demonstrate that in rural societies of developing countries (a) behavioral relations are utilized as insurance substitutes by providing a source of collaterals for credit, and (b) hir-ers of labor services modify or innovate labor contractual arrange-ments in order to efficiently manage farm production following the compulsions of the new technology. These are some of the common strands in existing literature that are developed in the following pages.

This book is primarily concerned with the unorganized markets of developing countries. One must recognize the possibility of informal markets also developing within public institutions of the formal sec-tor. Within the organized sector, if public monitoring of employees' conduct is weak, informal behavioral contracts can be resorted to by some members, through which well-organized corruption systems get established. So although the book follows the traditions of positive economics, it does recognize that behavioral relations are utilized equally to generate wealth by corrupt officials and criminal syndicates.

In Chapter 2 the theme of the book is developed so that the reader will be able to place many of the subliminal thoughts in their proper perspective, and the study is able to move on from generalities to specific issues.

Notes and References

1. Clifford Geertz, "The Bazaar Economy, Information and Change in Pleasant Marketing," *American Economic Review*, vol. 68, no. 2 (May 1978): 28–31.
2. The concept of a transition from status to contract has been elaborated by Sir Henry Summer Maine in *Ancient Law: Its Connection with Early History of Society, and Its Relations to Modern Ideas* (London: J. Murray & Co., 1981).
3. See Chapters 3 and 4 for discussion.
4. Polly Hill, *Migrant Cocoa Farmers of Southern Ghana* (New York: Cambridge University Press, 1970).
5. So far economists have neglected analyzing the qualitative aspects of poverty. Institutional aspects acquire significance if we are to understand how one-half of the population is able to survive at per capita income of $75 or less per annum. For quantitative estimates of poverty, see Hollis Chenery, with Ahluwalia, Bell, Duloy and Jolly, *Redistribution with Growth* (World Bank, 1983).
6. This book can be considered a generalized version of issues discussed in the rent-seeking literature. See Robert D. Tollison, "Rent Seeking: A Survey," *Kyklos*, vol. 35, fasc. 4 (1982): 575–602.
7. Anthony Giddens, *Capitalism and Modern Social Theory: An Analysis of the Writings of Marx, Durkheim and Max Weber* (New York: Cambridge University Press, 1971).
8. Armen A. Alchian and Harold Demsetz, "Production Information Costs and Economic Organization," *American Economic Review*, vol. 62, no. 5 (Dec. 1972): 777–795.
9. Harvey Liebenstein, "X-Efficiency: From Concept to Theory," *Challenge*, vol. 22 (Sept./Oct. 1979): 13–22; and "A Branch of Economics Is Missing: Micro-Macro Theory," *Journal of Economic Literature*, vol. 17 (June 1979): 477–502.
10. Benjamin Klein, Robert G. Crawford, and Armen A. Alchian, "Vertical Integration, Appropriable Rents and the Competitive Contracting Process," *Journal of Law and Economics*, vol. 21 (1978): 297–326.
11. Tollison, "Rent Seeking."

12. Yoram Ben Porath, "The F-Connection: Families, Friends and Firms and Organizations of Exchange," *Population and Development Review*, vol. 6, no. 1 (1980): 1–31.
13. Robert A. Pollak, "A Transaction Cost Approach to Families and Households," *Journal of Economic Literature*, vol. 23, no. 2 (June 1985): 581–608.
14. Hans P. Binswanger and Mark Rosenzweig, "Behavioral and Material Determinants of Production Relations in Agriculture," Discussion Paper No. 5, Research Unit, Agriculture and Rural Development Department, Operational Policy Staff (World Bank, 1982).

2

Informal Property Rights, Production, and Market Exchange

The creation and use of informal property rights in production and market exchange make up the sum and substance of this study. This chapter develops the conceptual tools that are used for analysis later.

The first section touches upon the ideas explored in the subsequent chapters. Following this, the second section explains the nature of property rights that are nurtured in unorganized markets. The third section lays out the logic of the study so that the reader is able to relate to the existing (and often tangentially relevant) literature, and pick up the main strands of argument developed in the pages to follow.

Behavioral Relations as Sources of Wealth Generation

In neoclassical economic analysis, wealth is generated either through production or through exchange. In the process of production inputs are combined to produce an output of higher value. During exchange also, goods and services are transferred to individuals who place a higher valuation on them. In this study a third dimension is proposed: that behavioral relations themselves, by creating expected utility, can act as sources of wealth generation during either production or exchange. The chapters that follow seek to demonstrate that these relations can be privately and often even socially productive.

A common strand of thought among economists covering a wide spectrum of ideology has been that the very poor, who account for about 40 percent of the population in many countries of Asia and Africa, are propertyless, atomistic individuals constituting an ignorant proletariat.[1] This study intends to show that for most of these individuals wealth often exists in the form of regular behavioral relations that acquire the characteristics of intangible property rights. Although the rights may not amount to much in tangible terms (relative to income levels in developed countries), they do constitute important sources of income and purchasing power, and play a major role in these persons' calculus of optimization.[2]

The object, then, is to understand the productivity of behavioral relations in unorganized markets of an economy. These invisible restrictions, which are administered either through existing norms and conventions of social groups, or alternatively by newly evolved conventions, can produce a whole range of wealth-generating informal institutions.[3]

The informal property rights or entitlements arise from two types of behavioral relations. First, individuals may be involved in hierarchical relations or vertical forms of exchange (often of a patron-client form with more affluent persons) during an economic transaction. In the modern context, such arrangements secure for participants economic benefits through a form of risk-pooling. These hierarchical relations in the unorganized sector have experienced considerable changes in recent decades. With changes in economic interests following the opening up of village markets, improvements in transport and communications, and spread of education, tradition-based exchange entitlements mappings (to use Sen's terminology) have steadily lost ground. In their place, however, new conventions have evolved as insurance mechanisms for hirers of labor services and hired labor to safeguard against the manifold uncertainties of markets exchange. Such uncertainties have arisen from (a) risk, (b) informational problems, and (c) weaknesses of the legal system. The emerging behavioral relations can be described as informal contracts designed to overcome institutional weaknesses of the unorganized sector during market exchange. These processes have enabled the poor to replace many fast-disappearing traditional entitlements with a new set of contracted economic rights.[4]

The second form of behavioral relations has involved horizontal forms of exchange within the informal groups, like the cocoa companies discussed in Chapter 1. In unorganized markets there are several opportunities for such groups to collectively acquire access to income or purchasing power. These sources of income can be tan-

gible objects (like the cocoa trees), or even intangible earning opportunities through restriction-seeking activities. As a collective ent-
ity a group can secure externalities in obtaining consumption credit
or employment—and even in production.[5]

The Nature of Extralegal Property Rights

The standard definition of property rights is "sanctioned behavioral
relations among men that arise from the existence of goods and per-
taining to their use."[6] This definition places on the legal system the
onus of both suitably defining and adequately protecting property
rights. The rights consequently acquire the characteristics of exclusive ownership and free transferability.[7]

Property rights need not arise exclusively from contracting via the
legal system. Any type of informal but self-policed contract between
individuals can equally well generate property rights, as illustrated
by the Ghanaian cocoa companies. In these situations exclusivity in
rights over resources is developed through self-policed contracts
without legal protection. Clearly there are important differences between property rights generated in this process and those generated
through the legal system. The principal differences are:

1. In extralegal property rights, transactions are made possible
   through informal contracts that are byproducts of conventions.
   The regularity in relations is maintained endogenously by the
   concerned parties rather than by court adjudication, so the contracts are self-policed.
2. Unlike legal property rights, where exclusivity of ownership is
   a necessary precondition before any market exchange, in extralegal property rights, as long as everyone follows the social
   norms, tangible resources can be privately put to productive use.
   Individuals can thus "arrange with others to combine resources
   in production and consumption and thereby create new uses
   for these resources" without recognition from the legal system.[8]
   This variant of property rights implies that through informal
   contracts individuals can acquire access to income streams from
   tangible resources even when there is no legal recognition.

In unorganized markets of today, individuals can also use behavioral relations to acquire access to what is essentially intangible property. The distinction between tangible and intangible property, to
quote Thorstein Veblen, is:

> Both are assets—that is to say, both are values determined by a
> capitalization of anticipated income yielding capacity. . . . The tan-

gible assets capitalize the preferential use of technological and industrial expedients . . . the preferential use being secured by the ownership of material articles employed in the processes in which these expedients are put into effect. The intangible assets capitalize the preferential use of certain facts of human nature—habits, propensities, beliefs, aspirations, necessities—to be dealt with under the psychological laws of human motivation.[9]

The best illustration of such property rights can be found in routine business transactions. If, for instance, a buyer of a good or service repeatedly transacts with the same seller because of convenience or satisfaction with the product, the latter begins to receive a steady stream of income from an essentially casual relation. Alternately, a group of individuals could agree to collectively restrict access of others to an earning opportunity, and thereby earn rents. In both cases the earning opportunity amounts to the generation of intangible property rights because (a) informal contractual relations ensure that earnings continue over successive time periods and (b) income is likely to include a rent component. Such intangible property rights arise out of invisible behavioral contracts and can be termed social assets.

Economists have not paid much attention to these forms of property rights for two reasons. First, intangible property rights are usually not recognized by the legal system, and so in a legal sense have never existed. Second, such contracts do not arise from tradable property rights and so do not have market values attached to them. For a casual observer, therefore, the property rights generated remain abstract concepts, although for individuals involved in the contracting processes the resultant rights are valued social assets.[10] An understanding of the taxonomy of such relations becomes important as a first step in incorporating these market forms into the conventional wisdom of development economics.

The Design of the Study

The next three chapters develop the theme of informal property rights, and describe how they are formed and protected in unorganized markets. The last four chapters are more concerned with the institutional and policy implications of such intangible property rights formation.

Figure 1 summarizes the contents of the next seven chapters. It attempts to provide a bird's-eye view of the main ideas discussed in this study. The basic distinction made is between property rights pro-

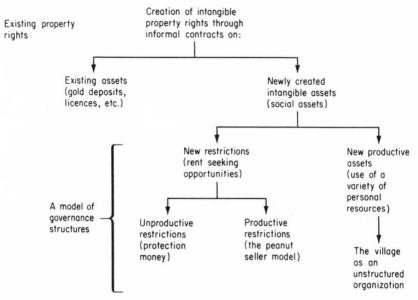

Figure 1. Understanding the Informal Sector.

tected by the formal legal system, and informal property rights protected by self-policed contracts.[11] These contracts are utilized to appropriate incomes from (a) existing assets or tangible resources such as land, gold mines, and cocoa trees; and (b) alternately intangible property rights or social assets.

Social assets in turn are generated in two ways. First *tied rents* are secured in hierarchical behavioral relations in labor markets. Second, by creating artificial restrictions, they permit the exploitation of rent-seeking opportunities. These can be either productive, as in some informal sector vocations, or socially unproductive when criminal syndicates or corrupt officials develop such rights.

Creation of Property Rights Through Informal Contracts

The basis of property rights, as discussed earlier, can be a system of informal behavioral contracts. Four variants of these contracts are possible in an economic system. These variants are: simple bilateral contracts, general bilateral contracts, simple multilateral contracts, and general multilateral contracts. Each of these forms is briefly explained below.[12]

Simple Bilateral Contracts

Two persons make a specific informal contract. For instance, a consumer purchases a product from a grocery store. The market exchange is in the form of an instantaneous contract that is negotiated and executed the moment the cash and the goods change hands. A change in objective conditions (say the product does not meet the buyer's expectations of quality), will lead to a cancellation of future transactions. Such contracts having very limited and specific purposes are termed *simple bilateral contracts.*

Neoclassical markets assume such relations among the actors in an economic system. Take labor markets. Labor is assumed to be hired as an atomistic factor of production only as long as its marginal product exceeds the wage. Even if labor finds employment on a daily basis, the process of finding work involves free and open competition with all other aspirants every day.[13]

Simple Multilateral Contracts

An individual or firm contracts with a large number of people through bilateral contracts. The presence of a number of buyers gives the seller reasonable chance of repeated behavioral relations. While each transaction by itself is a simple bilateral relation, the size and/or repeated nature of transactions gives sellers steady streams of income, with some flexibility for marginal adjustments in their earnings. Accounts describe the intangible assets created as goodwill. Simple bilateral and multilateral contracts are discussed in Chapter 6.

General Bilateral Contracts

Unlike simple bilateral relations, these relations involve complex patterns of contracting. In the earlier example, the grocer is also the buyer's uncle, village moneylender, and a locally elected official.

Such complex relations need not involve just members of a family but they acquire importance, as discussed earlier, in the unorganized sector where requirements of labor are unique for each hirer.[14] A combination of traits and qualities such as trustworthiness, reliability, and capability for sustained effort levels may be able to earn tied rents. In these situations the hirers and the hired contract with each other at multiple levels in their bilateral relationships, and in the process pool their risks. Behavioral relations consequently become socially and privately productive.

The reason hirers of labor services need such arrangements is that several production risks arise from (a) the compulsions of modern technology in agriculture and (b) the nature of adapted technology in urban informal sector enterprises. These risks place a premium on labor willing to make the requisite behavioral adjustments and physical effort.[15]

Of course, the exact distribution of the additional wealth created between the two parties will depend on their relative bargaining strengths. At one end of the scale, relations could be highly exploitative when the power equations are asymmetrical. At the other end of the scale, labor may have some forms of countervailing power, either because of production risks faced by hirers of its services or because of labor market segmentation. While the exact nature of these contractual relations will vary from case to case, some concepts can be developed to explain how labor acquires countervailing power.

General Multilateral Contracts

Here multilateral relations extend across a group of people. Within the group all members have multilateral relations with one another. The best examples of such contracting arrangements can be found in family-run production units, such as a small restaurant. While the spouses take care of the cooking and accounting, children may be working as unpaid waiters and waitresses. Even larger groups such as clans, castes, and tribes have often utilized their existing conventions to achieve their group interests.

General multilateral relations imply that each person within the group is interacting with every other person at several levels of behavioral relations. This can arise only if the group collectively is able to identify an interest that does not conflict with the members' individual interests.[16]

Three forms of general multilateral contracts are visualized where free-rider problems are less likely to emerge.[17] First, in an anarchic situation a group may be compelled to stand together and use its collective strength defensively to maintain exclusive control over a resource or income stream, as the cocoa entrepreneurs in Ghana were forced to do. In Chapter 5 a simple model is developed on these lines to demonstrate how groups maintain control over public locations in the urban informal sector.

Second, general multilateral contracts could be the only means by which indivisibilities in a production process can be overcome. For instance, informal cooperation is often necessary in agriculture in the form of farmers supplying each other with voluntary labor during the harvesting season, or jointly managing irrigation of their lands.[18] Alternately, these relations could perform the role of insurance substitutes, with groups spreading out risks among all members.

Third, when peer groups maintain such behavioral relations, they usually have perfect knowledge of each person's work and effort capabilities. So informal groups can be made to serve an institutional function of efficiently screening job seekers in unorganized labor markets.

In all three situations, general multilateral contracts facilitate group action, and deadweight losses in different production activities are reduced.[19]

Informal Contracts on Existing Assets

If tangible property rights are not recognized by the legal system, individuals can always resort to original contracts whenever net benefits from these arrangements are perceived to be adequate. John Umbeck, in a fascinating study of the California Gold Rush of the nineteenth century, has documented such contracting processes.[20] He describes the methods by which gold prospectors in California arranged mutually advantageous contracts to stake their claims on prospecting areas, at a time when the long arm of the law had not reached them. The contracts, like the ones executed by Ghanaian companies, served a limited objective of building up group strength to keep intruders away by achieving "economies of scale in violence." The groups contracted with each other solely for their collective security, and individual prospectors privately appropriated wealth by panning for gold on their individually staked territories.

Such informal contracts can also enable individuals to stake claims on public resources and rents arising out of public policy, a theme discussed in Chapter 8.

Newly Created Intangible Assets (Social Assets)

New Restrictions

When general multilateral contracts are utilized by groups, entry access is limited to non-group members, and opportunities to earn rents may be created. One can view group members as earning varying amounts of economic rents. Such restrictions could be either productive or unproductive.

Productive restrictions of this form often arise in the unorganized markets of the Urban Informal Sector. Restrictions can be considered productive whenever (a) they create endogenous informal institutions through which a whole range of inexpensive urban services are provided and every potential income stream available in a city is appropriated, and (b) they allow small business enterprises to survive and compete in highly unstable business environments.

Many such restrictions could also be unproductive. Criminal organizations often create restrictions and extort protection money. A considerable range of public corruption is also of this form.

New Productive Assets

Apart from using general multilateral contracts to secure rent-seeking opportunities, the poor can also create new intangible productive assets by engaging in general bilateral contracts. This feature has become relevant because of the compulsions of technology following the green revolution. The phenomenon of interlocked markets observed in rural areas is suggested to have led to the generation of new endogenous institutional mechanisms by which rural labor has been able to earn tied rents in exchange for providing a desired level of quality and efficiency of labor services.

The informal rights in these two categories of contracting are qualitatively different. When restriction seeking takes place through general multilateral contracts, existing conventions or structural features of peer groups generate positive externalities that in turn secure access to income. In general bilateral contracts, by contrast, behavioral relations are more hierarchical, often simultaneously evolving and utilizing conventions through which the two parties are able to pool their risks. Clearly, both make behavioral relations productive.

Existing Property Rights Literature

Property rights analysts have so far been concerned only with analyzing how legally recognized tangible property rights are utilized in an economic system. Their assumption, relevant for developed countries with efficient institutions, is that the law is always enforced. In a developing country, enforcement of the law is often inefficient and incomplete. This distinction between efficient and inefficient enforcement becomes important because, even for tangible property, inefficient enforcement mechanisms may force property owners to resort to informal contracts in order to protect their property rights. Efficient enforcement of laws and administrative regulations takes place in the relatively smaller organized sector, and among property owners in urban areas.

Efficient Enforcement

This is the main strand of property rights literature. Work by Williamson, Alchian and Demsetz, Coase, and others has made impressive contributions toward the understanding of industrial organizations and the forms of interaction between law and economics.

The underlying assumption in all these studies is that the legal system functions efficiently. For this the system should have the following properties. First, there should be an established body of property and tort law.[21] The legal system then develops and defines property rights and specifies a set of appropriate rules when these rights are exchanged. Second, and of equal importance, there must be an efficient process of enforcement of legal rights by the judicial and administrative system. When these conditions are satisfied, markets function efficiently, with well-defined property rights for buyers and sellers. Efficiency therefore implies that not only should legal rights and interests be suitably defined, but they must be adequately protected by the state.

Once these conditions are met, the only institutional costs that arise are transactions costs. These costs can then be conveniently included as another constraint in an optimization process for consumption or production.

Inefficient Enforcement

Inefficient enforcement of law results in the attenuation of even a person's tangible property rights. For instance, an average civil court in India has jurisdiction over 800,000 individuals, a police station is responsible for over 100,000 persons. Costs of administering the system for such large populations are so high that a considerable number of the grievances of law abiding citizens will have to remain unattended to.

A landowner with a medium-sized holding will have to wait quite a while for legal redress against encroachment on his land. Litigation in property relations is taken to civil courts that are extremely slow in disposal of cases. Costs are high, in terms of both time and lawyer's fees. Unless the landowner has the right connections in the administration, the costs of maintaining his rights will be very high.[22]

The cost of maintaining exclusivity forces the landowner to resort to informal contracts. He may find it more convenient to establish enduring relations with some of the landless or marginal cultivators in the village in order to overcome these handicaps. Land is leased out or given as sharecropping tenure to the latter, and in return the landlord's entire property is efficiently policed. Such arrangements can also be viewed as generating social assets for the poor.

One might argue that in the above example labor is functioning as a private police force. This is, however, not entirely correct. The inefficiencies of the legal system prevent the landowner from turning to a private police because such simple bilateral contracting systems are difficult to execute. A person has to evolve a set of complex interlinked relations that lead to different forms of tenancy. The study, however, does not deal with such forms of informal property rights because existing analysis on sharecropping and other forms of tenancy can easily incorporate this factor as just another dimension of risk for a landowner.[23]

Organization of Chapters

The next three chapters analyze the major features of intangible property rights not recognized by the legal system. Chapter 3 examines the inducements for such contracting processes, and seeks to define the exact nature of these informal property rights in the traditions of institutional economics.

Chapters 4 and 5 analyze the nature of informal contracting processes in unorganized markets under two broad subdivisions covering economic activities in the rural sector, and in the urban informal sector. As the scope of study is vast, covering both product and factor markets, attention is confined only to examining contractual arrangements in markets where the poor secure earning opportunities. Apart from labor markets, where many of the poor find work, institutions governing markets for consumption credit, street hawking, future property rights, and slum housing are also analyzed. Wherever possible the arguments are supported with evidence from relevant studies, but as data are not always available, some sections of these chapters tend to be more speculative than others. Chapter 4 examines rural contracts and looks at the opportunity costs for people who engage in informal contracts in labor and consumption credit markets. These contracting alternatives are hypothesized to be greatly influenced by the institution of a village, which not only segments labor markets but also provides a set of contracting options for the poor. The chapter seeks to provide an alternate explanation for the concept of interlocked markets.

Chapter 5 focuses attention on urban informal contracts. Unlike rural contracts, with urban contracts there is no exogenous institution like a village to segment markets. Instead, groups acquire access to earning opportunities by devising endogenous institutions, resulting in interesting implications for labor market segmentation.

The next section of the book focuses on the secondary level of these behavioral relations. As was discussed earlier, such relations outline the contours of informal institutions that dictate access to income and employment opportunities.

Chapter 6 completes the discussion of extralegal property rights and seeks to describe how these informal institutions enrich the understanding of market governance structures. A model of institutional governance structures is formulated that incorporates some ideas developed in the earlier chapters.

Chapter 7 examines the implications of this study for understanding rural-urban migration decisions of the poor. Migrants, it is suggested, attempt to maximize a portfolio of tangible and intangible property rights.

Chapter 8 examines the way informal contracting processes can be used to explain the formation of corruption systems in developing countries.

Chapter 9 summarizes the major implications of this study. After briefly summarizing the analysis of previous chapters, a suggestion is made to include social assets in the conventional wisdom of development economics. Following this, a brief discussion is undertaken on policies and prospects with regard to social entitlements. Finally, Chapter 9 draws down the curtain with a summing up of the institutional consequences of these contracting processes.

Conclusion

Informal contracts create exclusivity in individuals' dealings with each other, and consequently enable them to generate and partition income streams. Two features stand out in analyzing these social assets. First, as the assets are not easily transferable, one cannot visualize markets in them. Second, any individual in a system may possess, or invest nonfinancial resources in developing, these assets, implying that even the poorest of the poor can have a portfolio of these assets. One can conclude that opportunity costs of labor in very poor societies need not be zero as postulated by many development economists. In fact, the distribution of social assets may take a form completely different from the distribution of conventional tangible assets.

These informal contracting process require a reassessment of the nature of unorganized sector markets in developing countries. Virtually all markets are segmented through restriction-seeking activities of individuals and groups, and a whole range of informal institutions is created at different levels of economic activity. An understanding of these institutions can perhaps fill in some missing links of development economics literature.

Notes and References

1. Arthur W. Lewis, "Economic Development with Unlimited Supply of Labour," *Manchester School of Economics and Social Studies*, vol. 22 (May 1954): 329–402. Also G. Ranis and J. C. H. Fei, "A Theory of Economic Development," *American Economic Review*, vol. 51, no. 4 (1961): 531–565. For the Marxist approach, see Samir Amin, *Imperialism and Unequal Development* (New York: Monthly Review Press, 1977).
2. Income levels and purchasing power in developing countries have been extensively analyzed, but these studies have invariably ignored the wealth-generating role of informal institutions. For the best known of such studies see Irving B. Kravis with Alan Heston, Robert Summers, and Alicia Civitello, *International Comparison of Real Product and Purchasing Power* (Baltimore: Johns Hopkins University Press, 1978).
3. For an analysis of conventions see Harvey Liebenstein, "On the Economics of Conventions and Institutions: An Exploratory Survey," in *Journal of Institutional and Theoretical Economics*, vol. 140 (1980): 74–86. Liebenstein describes how conventions are utilized during economic exchange to obtain (a) search advantage, (b) coordination advantage, and (c) prisoner's dilemma avoidance advantage. These advantages amount to informal property rights whenever they generate regular income streams. Also see Andrew Schotter, *An Economic Theory of Institutions* (New York: Cambridge University Press, 1980), for a game-theoretic analysis of these issues.
4. In a traditional society, entitlement mappings are determined by social norms and conventions. A. K. Sen has emphasized the entitlements aspect of poverty while analyzing the Great Bengal Famine of 1942. Amartya K. Sen, *Poverty and Famine: An Essay on Entitlement and Deprivation* (New

York: Oxford University Press, 1981). Also Amartya K. Sen, *Poverty and Unemployment in India: An Analysis of Recent Evidence* (World Bank Staff Working Paper No. 417, 1980).

5. Members of a group could be clansmen, kinsmen, caste members, or just a collection of individuals having similar structural interests. In these groupings existing conventions and norms resolve conflicts, thereby reducing danger of the free-rider problem.

6. Eirik G. Furubotn and S. Pejovich, *The Economics of Property Rights* (Cambridge: Ballinger Publishing Co., 1974). The word "sanctioned" implies a well-defined and legally enforced penalty system for violations of these norms.

7. Bruce Ackerman, ed., *Economic Analysis of Property Law* (Boston: Little, Brown & Co., 1975). The freedom to transfer through market exchange ensures that on a voluntary basis resources get diverted to activities yielding the highest returns.

8. John Umbeck, *A Theory of Property Rights* (Ames: Iowa State University Press, 1981), p. 4.

9. Thorstein Veblen, "On the Nature of Capital, Intangible Assets and the Pecuniary Magnate," *Quarterly Journal of Economics*, vol. 22 (1908): 104–136. The quotation is from page 116.

10. Affluent persons have also benefited through such contracts. In the organized sector tangible resources are invested to nurture and protect these rights.

11. For a useful summary on forms of property rights see Louis De Alessi, "Survey on Property Rights Literature," in Richard O. Zerbe, ed., *Research in Law and Economics*, vol. 2 (Greenwich: Jai Press, 1980), pp. 1–44.

12. These terms are generalizations of the terms Simplex and Multiplex relations. See Robert Kidder, *Connecting Law and Society* (Englewood Cliffs: Prentice-Hall, 1983). Kidder argues that a transition from multiplex to simplex relations takes place when the legal system becomes efficiently organized. Our categorization has included two additional terms to take into account the possibility that multiperson behavioral relations can be equally important in a society.

13. Of course, qualitative uncertainties in labor markets can change the nature of this process even in simple bilateral relations. New institutions evolve and perform the role of screening and certification in organized markets to circumvent this problem.

14. In unorganized labor markets behavioral traits may be as important as job skills in organized labor markets.

15. All labor may not be willing to make such behavioral adjustments because some contracting options are available to them. See Chapter 4.

16. The study by Richard Posner, "A Theory of Primitive Society," *Journal of Law and Economics*, vol. 33, no. 1 (April 1980), has analyzed related issues in a society where legal institutions are underdeveloped. In this study, by contrast, informal contracting processes are analyzed in an economy with widespread prevalence of market exchange.

17. Mancur Olson, *Logic of Collective Action* (Cambridge: Harvard University Press, 1971), for related discussion on the free-rider problem.

18. E. Walter Coward, Jr., "Principles of Social Organization in an Indigenous Irrigation System," *Human Organization*, vol. 38, no. 1 (1978): 28–46.
19. This feature is being recognized by institutional economists and organizational theorists studying production organization in the Far East. See William G. Ouchi and Raymond Price, "Hierarchies, Clans and Theory Z: A New Perspective on Organization Development," *Organizational Dynamics* (Autumn 1978): 25–44.
20. John Umbeck, *Property Rights*. Such contracts can also take place within public organizations, leading to corruption systems.
21. Richard Posner, *Economic Analysis of Law* (Boston: Little, Brown & Co., 1980).
22. Oliver Mendelsohn, "Pathology of the Indian Legal System," *Modern Asian Studies*, vol. 15 (1981): 823–864, describes the problems of enforcing property rights when a retired army officer decided to return to his village in Rajasthan, India, and start self-cultivation on his private land.
23. For a survey of literature on share-cropping, see M. G. Quibria, "The Puzzle of Sharecropping: A Survey of Recent Evidence," *World Development*, vol. 12, no. 2 (Feb. 1984): 103–114.

3

Toward a Theory of Social Assets

The definition of property rights has taken many forms in the history of human civilization. It is however only in the last few decades, following the seminal work of Coase that economists have begun extensively analyzing the implications of legally recognized property rights.[1] Significant contributions have been made toward understanding the concepts of externalities, contracting processes, and the nature of business organizations.

This chapter inquires into the properties of intangible property rights not recognized by the legal system. The first section examines the factors that lead to the formation of such rights. The next section analyzes the nature of these rights using the framework of property rights literature. Following this, some implications for understanding contracting processes are discussed in the final section of the chapter.

The Inducements for Intangible Property Rights

Informal property rights can have their roots traced to original contracts executed outside the legal system. These contracts function as insurance mechanisms for the poor by affording steady earning opportunities. When a person utilizes such implicit contracts he does not have to be totally dependent on the uncertainties of a daily wage market. Obviously, there have to be equally convincing reasons why the relatively affluent (buyers of these services) find such contracts useful. In this section, the inducements of both parties to such contracts are discussed.

Three main causal factors can be identified for such contract formation. In any society the mere presence of conventions and status relationships may define a recurrent pattern of contact between individuals during market exchange. Alternately, in the modern market system, compulsions of technology or informational constraints could generate new conventions that safeguard a set of behavioral relations. Finally, institutional weaknesses of formal organizations and public policies could also give rise to informal contracting processes. Of the three, the first two forms perform important functions in generating wealth for the poor in production and in market exchange.

Traditional Factors

Since prehistory societies have organized themselves by weaving together an intricate pattern of social norms, which lay out conditions for social relations between individuals and groups. Two conditions allow these norms to acquire stability. First, the norms should become a part of each individual's personality—be *internalized*. Second, a sanctions system has to devise procedures by which conformity to the norms is rewarded and deviations are punished. This process is termed *institutionalization*.[2] Once norms are internalized and institutionalized, the behavioral relations themselves provide a mechanism for informal contracting without taking recourse to formal laws of contract. This implies that in groups with well-laid-out customary norms, any visible pattern of exchange entitlements can also be viewed as the result of informal, self-policed contracting processes.

In fact, as Sen has pointed out, in traditional societies all members of the community secured an exchange entitlements mapping through such customary norms. Rights and obligations afforded every individual a set of economic entitlements from the rest of the community.[3] The actual set of entitlements became equal or unequal among different members depending on how the society had evolved over time.

Some, like the Hindu caste system, were hierarchical, with status privileges diminishing as one moved down the hierarchy. These were conveniently translated into highly unequal entitlements for different members of the caste system. Many similar illustrations can be recounted from the past and the present, where a few patrons and many clients coexisted in a symbiotic relationship.

With the spread of markets, however, hierarchical forms have had difficulty in surviving because the patrons became increasingly conscious of the economic value of their tangible property rights, while gradually neglecting their social obligations. Hierarchical relations based on customary norms gradually ceased to offer entitlements to the poor.

A breakdown of these customary norms has not, however, driven all the poor into a restless reserve army of the unemployed because their erstwhile patrons, as well as a rising class of noveau riche, have needed to cement new informal contracts as risk-pooling arrangements during market exchange. The resultant informal institutions have been protected by conventions arising out of economic factors, instead of traditional conventions. Such arrangements have created new sets of contracting options for the poor, to be discussed in the next section.

In contrast to "traditional" bilateral contracts of patron-client relations, general multilateral relations within social groups have often continued to survive and, in fact, sometimes flourished in a modern market system. Behavioral relations within such groups, policed by established conventions and norms, have in unorganized markets been utilized to appropriate earning opportunities. Successful family-run enterprises are one such illustration. There have also been instances of larger groups utilizing their informal organizations to generate significant externalities in production.

Janet Landa has documented the Chinese use of clan conventions in Malaysia to run business and industry. Clan norms facilitated cost-less implicit contracts between group members in production and trading activities in the market economy.[4] These clans were able to utilize existing behavioral relations among members to execute contracts with minimum transactions costs. If for instance, a business-person X needed $100,000 urgently to tide over a cash-flow problem, he could borrow it from his clan member Y without collaterals or formal contracts.

In an analogous manner many of the poor in developing countries today are often able to use group conventions to appropriate economic benefits. Customary groupings like castes, tribes, or kinship groups are utilized productively, to generate wealth through restriction-seeking activities.

Economic Factors

Labor markets in developing countries are usually far removed from the smoothly operating institutions assumed by neoclassical economies. Both hirers of labor services and hired labor face several individual risks. For hirers, the risks during production are aggravated by the absence of institutional mechanisms that could insure them adequately. For hired labor, the risk arises from uncertainties in finding adequate employment in daily-wage labor markets. In these situations general bilateral contracts allow both parties to pool their risks. The risk factor for the hirers will be analyzed for the farm sector and urban informal sector separately.

Since the 1960s the agricultural sector or rural farm sector has been reaping the benefits of a technology oriented toward biotechnology rather than mechanotechnology.[5] In other words, agricultural output has been increased by intensive use of hybrid seeds, fertilizers, water, and pesticides rather than by labor-saving machines. These inputs need sizable financial investments by farmers, and their success depends a great deal on correct time-sequenced farming operations. Farmers consequently need to devise suitable labor management strategies so that the requirements of the technology are adequately met.

Take, for instance, rice technology today. An intricate sequence of farm operations is necessary to cover almost the whole cropping season. At each stage reliable and experienced labor is essential.[6] Multiple cropping practices have further increased the duration of requirement of services of such labor. Informal bilateral contracts with some workers can ensure that at certain critical time spans managerial risk of lack of reliable labor is eliminated. In these situations, landowners and labor pool their risks and secure increases in productivity and economic welfare. Labor's share of the increased wealth will depend on several factors that will be discussed in the next two chapters.

In urban areas, the situation in the unorganized or urban informal sector is equally interesting.[7] Labor in these activities is required on a regular basis, and the behavioral component acquires importance because effort levels and adaptability of employees play a role as critical as that of job skills in organized sector employment systems.

Take, for instance, a small entrepreneur who needs to hire labor for a typical low-return informal vocation like a cycle repair shop. The important feature that distinguishes his enterprise from the neoclassical firm is that limited capital equipment has to be continuously adapted and adjusted to secure maximum returns. The scarcity of fixed and working capital calls for high levels of adaptability and effort among all employees. Here again, as in the rural sector, some workers willingly adjust behavioral relations and secure steady employment in the firms.

Labor's countervailing power in these situations will exhibit a great deal of diversity. If, as is usually the case, these hired workers socialize in customary groups such as clans, tribes, or castes, employers also find it convenient to utilize their existing informal social networks as screening mechanisms for job vacancies in order to avoid adverse selections during new recruitment. When job openings arise in the enterprise, these groups are tacitly allowed to screen job seekers. Obviously, people with access to such groups will be the only ones who secure job openings. Labor markets consequently get segmented.[8]

These contractual arrangements are variants of von Weizsacker's extrapolation principle.[9] Weizsacker argues that buyers extrapolate market relations on the basis of past experience, preferring to return to the same seller as long as opportunity costs of searching elsewhere are higher. In the example of the cycle repair shop, the employer extrapolates the quality of a new worker on the basis of experience he has already obtained working with an informal group. The workers also use a predictable behavior and thereby reduce their risk of dismissal.

Apart from factor markets, where specific behavioral relations may earn remunerations or tied rents, general multilateral relations among groups are also utilized in product markets to gain access to income streams whenever the attendant free-rider problems can be resolved. For instance, urban markets often develop in certain areas because of locational convenience. Buyers return to demand goods and services because the site (a busy bus stand or railway station) is convenient. An informal group in such cases may be able to utilize its collective strength as a part of its production technology and appropriate the locational rents.[10]

To sum up, in the unorganized sector economic factors often lead to informal contracting processes. These create among the labor force new forms of entitlements, or access to entitlements. General bilateral relations enable hirers to partition their income streams in exchange for labor of desired quality and reliability. Alternatively, groups may be able to exploit positive externalities by using existing conventions in production. In both cases, regular behavioral relations lead to a steady generation of income over time. When behavioral relations have such a productive element, they can be described as social assets.

Public Policy

A third inducement for informal contracting processes arises from administrative regulations, and from the structure of modern business organizations. The former aspect has been analyzed by the rent-seeking literature.[11] Economists have shown that when public policy imposes restrictions through quotas, permits, and rationing systems, resources are wasted by individuals attempting to seek rent.

This study suggests that rent-seeking activities in rural communities play an important direct role in defining the contracting capabilities of the poor. Affluent villagers contract with the poor, and the latter are allowed consumption credit in exchange for mortgaging their current or future property rights from governmental programs.[12]

Apart from public policies, structural weaknesses in formal organizations can also lead to contracting possibilities by which individuals acquire and partition income streams by selling favors in illegal markets.[13] Corruption can thus be viewed as a result of the creation of informal property rights through such contracts.

Social Assets as a Form of Property Rights

The informal contracting processes induced by the traditional or economic factors discussed result in the productivity of behavioral relations, which in turn generate income streams. These relations lead to a form of property rights when the income generated is recurring over time, and thus has a measure of permanence. In this section the exact nature of such intangible property rights is discussed using the framework of law and economics.

Literature on property rights has been mainly concerned with rights derived from property recognized by law. The emphasis has been on examining forms of ownership, and their resulting implications for economic analysis.

There has been an attempt to identify three major types of ownership rights.[14] These are:

1. *Usus*: This constitutes a right to simply use an asset. An example of such a right would be the rights of a worker in a competitive firm. He or she has the right to use machines and equipment supplied by the firm during the production process. Another example could be an individual's right to use a bench or picnic table in a public park. The concept could be equally applied to employees in state-owned enterprises.
2. *Usus fructus*: In this form the right to use is modified to include the right to enjoy any income flow generated by the asset. Some

constraints are, however, imposed on the user. First, the quality of the asset (stock) should not be allowed to deteriorate. If there is any deterioration in value, the user has to provide for the depreciation. Second, the right is not transferable. The individual can improve the asset but cannot capitalize the value. Finally, the user is given terminable ownership of the asset. Whenever the owner decides to terminate the right (of course following legal procedures) the user ceases to enjoy the usufruct. A typical example of this is the worker in a Yugoslav worker-managed firm.

3. *Abusus*: This right is all-encompassing, allowing a person to change an asset's form and substance in addition to the first two rights. The term "well-defined property rights" in the neoclassical sense refers to such rights. In market exchange, economists normally assume the existence of this form of property rights.

Informal contracting processes result in a variant of category 2, or usufructuary rights. It will be useful therefore to examine some properties of such rights. In legal terminology a person acquiring usufructuary rights is able to maintain only *de facto* control over the property. The *de jure* control (having title to the property) remains with the owners. So a usufruct can be enjoyed only when the essential character of the property is not altered. A sharecropper, for instance, can cultivate a plot of land, but he cannot build on it, say, a household dwelling.

In many traditional societies resources have been shared by a community as usufructuary rights. Jodha, has discussed how community pastures in Rajasthan (India) were grazed by livestock belonging to all villagers.[15] "Communal" tenures of African farming systems similarly allowed all members of a tribe to acquire land rights.[16] Such usufructuary rights could function effectively as long as society had, through its conventions, defined the exact nature of the usufruct. In Rajasthan the feudal landlord administered these properties. In Western Africa, tribal elders or chiefs performed a similar role. With the pressure of population and technological change these usufructuary rights have gradually degenerated and disappeared. The phrase "the tragedy of the commons" has been used to describe this process.[17]

The argument put forth here is that usufructuary rights can also arise on intangible property protected by implicit contracts. These rights can be termed as social usufructuary rights.

The important features of social usufructuary rights are basically threefold. First, these rights, as with all usufructuary rights, are not tradable. A person appropriating the usufruct cannot capitalize the value of these assets.[18] Second, unlike normal usufructuary rights, there are no *de jure* or allodial owners of these rights. All persons involved in these informal contracts collectively possess these rights. If the informal grouping disappears, these rights also quickly vanish. Third, another distinctive feature of social usufructuary rights is that they receive no legal recognition or legal protection. Instead, they are self-policed and protected by contracted individuals themselves who utilize existing conventions or create new conventions for one of the reasons discussed in the earlier section. An endogenous sanctions system therefore replaces property and tort laws to administer such rights.

To sum up, an economic system can have several forms of original and derived social usufructuary rights. Some of these are listed below.

1. Sociological factors, economic factors, or public policy can lead to informal contracts through general bilateral relations, general multilateral relations, or simple multilateral relations in a market system. These give rise to a set of original social usufructuary rights.
2. Simple bilateral relations can also lead to a form of original social usufructuary rights when hirers of labor in job markets screen job applicants on the basis of credentials. Educational institutions granting these credentials acquire a form of such rights. Individuals in such cases seek out credentials in order to strengthen their claims for job property rights.
3. In a traditional economy, with reciprocity rather than market exchange, social conventions and customary norms may define social usufructuary rights. These rights determine the mapping of exchange entitlements for all members of the society.

Implications for Transactions Costs Analysis

Informal contracting processes have interesting implications for understanding transactions costs. As the analysis has indicated, these contracts are formulated and self-policed by the concerned parties instead of being administered by the legal system. There are no transactions costs in the usual sense of the term. In fact, an existing contractual arrangement could facilitate the formulation of several new contracts without associated transactions costs. In these situations transactions costs become functions of informal contracting processes and not functions of the legal liability system, as suggested by the traditions of law and economics.[19]

Two examples, one from India and one from the Sudan are briefly discussed in order to illustrate this point. The example from India is for the bidi, or country cigar, industry, and the example from the Sudan is from the Gezira Irrigation Scheme.

The Bidi Industry of Murshidabad

Some entrepreneurs found the villages of Murshidabad district in West Bengal (India) ideally suited for the bidi industry. This was because the manufacture of bidi is a very labor-intensive activity requiring manual rolling of tobacco in a special type of leaf. This area was considered suitable because of its proximity to major markets in India and Bangladesh, as well as the availability of cheap labor.[20]

More than cheap labor, production of bidis requires strict supervision because if a bidi is not rolled properly, and has too little or too much tobacco, market demand can shift quickly to another brand. Quality control of a highly labor-intensive process becomes a critical factor. The entrepreneurs circumvented this problem by appointing key members of local village elite as their contractors. These persons used their general bilateral contracts with agricultural laborers, as well as general multilateral relations among village groups to build up elaborate informal institutions which enabled production and quality inspection at minimum transactions cost.

The Gezira Scheme

The Gezira Scheme in the Sudan involved opening up vast tracts of the desert to cotton cultivation through irrigation by the Nile River. Because of the reluctance of Sudanese peasant families to offer their services in the labor markets, the initial demand for labor greatly exceeded labor supply at the inception of the project in 1925. The British colonial administrators overcame this problem by inducting groups of the Fulani tribe from Nigeria. These tribal groups were housed in relative isolation in exclusively Fulani settlements in the project area, and were encouraged to maintain their traditional social groupings. The groups obviously had elaborate networks of conventions through which all members could be controlled and utilized for various stages of cotton cultivation. O'Brien suggests that local Sudanese farmers were able to utilize the dependable Fulani labor for many decades to produce a very profitable cash crop. The system was, however, very exploitative, with these laborers not receiving any wage increases for four decades.[21]

The two examples discussed illustrate how, even in a "traditional" or colonial environment, behavioral relations have been utilized so that existing conventions have guaranteed production at minimum transactions costs. These traditional social assets were usually highly exploitative, as workers had virtually no countervailing power.

In the final chapter it is suggested that if public policy tries to utilize behavioral relations imaginatively, many analogous income sources are feasible for the poor. Such arrangements provide informal institutional alternatives to the concept of an integrated firm. In fact, such organizational designs have already been put to effective use in some Far Eastern countries for large-scale subcontracting.[22]

The interrelation between transactions costs and informal contracting processes also gives some new perspectives to the Coase Theorem. According to this theorem, if (a) property rights are well defined, and (b) transactions costs are zero, a perfectly competitive system will be allocationally efficient. The analysis in subsequent chapters indicate, that although informal contracting processes segment markets, they can maintain allocational efficiency within segments. This feature is possible because within segments positive externalities are generated by maintaining a desired pattern of behavioral relations without transactions costs.

If we take the Coasian example of a farmer who has a rancher as a neighbor, even if the two individuals do not have their property rights clearly demarcated, they may be able to resolve their externality problem (cattle straying into the farm and destroying crops) because of common interest cemented by existing informal behavioral relations. In rural India cowherds and shepherds have lived among agriculturists in this manner for centuries in many village communities.

The point of interest here is that while transactions costs within groups are lower, between groups they continue to be high. Unlike the Coasian framework, in a less-developed country the economic system as a whole is not a smoothly functioning competitive model. High transactions costs between groups imply that economic exchange between groups or segments may have varying degrees of inefficiency. Benefits of economic growth could therefore have very uneven spreads across different segments of the population.

Conclusion

The ideas discussed in this chapter have several interesting consequences for analysis. Most economists have assumed a clear distinction between property owners and the propertyless in developing countries. The lack of access to tangible property for the latter group makes them a part of a large reservoir of unemployed and underemployed labor force. Economists have then sought to demonstrate how these people fare during economic development. For instance, economists like Sir Arthur Lewis, Gustav Ranis, and John Fei demonstrate that these workers can be used as an inexpensive source of labor for rapid industrialization. Radical economists in the Marxian traditions, in contrast, argue that propertyless labor constitutes a class of unemployed people. The only solution to the massive surplus labor problem is to restructure the economy by state control of property rights.

Both these approaches are simplistic because they do not take into account the complex system of informal property rights that arises out of implicit contracting arrangements. These property rights generate wealth, segment markets, provide incentive mechanisms, and channel incomes among citizens in ways that are quite different from what received paradigms predict. The next six chapters present the different dimensions of these processes.

In conclusion, informal property rights emerge when behavioral relations have degrees of permanence in the economic system. For contracted individuals, these relations amount to social assets that may be as valuable as physical, financial, and human capital. These rights, in addition, alter a market's penalty-reward system. In contrast, for individuals left out of these processes, the system offers no opportunity of securing employment in labor markets. Destitution for such genuinely propertyless individuals is a stark reality.

Notes and References

1. See R. Coase, "The Problem of Social Cost," in *Journal of Law and Economics,* vol. 13 (Oct. 1960): 1–44.

2. See Karl Dieter Opp, "The Emergence and Effects of Social Norms: Confrontation of Some Hypotheses of Sociology and Economics," in *Kyklos*, vol. 32, fasc. 4 (1979): 775–801, for an explanation of these ideas.

3. See Pauline Mahar Kolenda, "Toward a Model of the Hindu Jajmani System," in *Tribal and Peasant Societies*, edited by George Dalton (Austin: University of Texas Press, 1967). Also see Andre Beteille, *Inequality among Men* (Oxford: Basil Blackwell, 1977), for a discussion of these concepts in relation to India.

4. See Janet T. Landa, "Theory of Ethnically Homogeneous Middlemen Group: Institutional Alternative to Contract Law," in the *Journal of Legal Studies*, vol. 10 (1981).

5. Stephen D. Biggs and Edward J. Clay, *Generation and Diffusion of Agricultural Technology: A Review of Theories and Experiences*, International Labour Office, Geneva, 1983 (WEP research working papers), summarize the leading issues in this area of research.

6. A recent article discusses the complexities faced by farmers adopting the new technology input packages. There are dozens of hybrid seed varieties, fifteen or sixteen varieties of insecticides and fertilizers, from which a farmer has to select his input package. Labor has to be trained for specific cultural practices. See Grace E. Goodell, "Bugs, Bunds, Banks and Bottlenecks: Organization Contradictions in the New Rice Technology," *Economic Development and Cultural Change*, vol. 33, no. 1 (Oct. 1984). The management of labor becomes as important as for the personnel manager in a modern factory! Another source giving an exhaustive account of Punjab agriculture is G. S. Bhalla and G. K. Chadha, *Green Revolution and the Small Peasant* (New Delhi: Concept Publishing Co., 1983).

7. Clifford Geertz, "The Bazaar Economy," discusses similar issues for a bazaar economy in Morocco. Geertz argues that "clientelization" is a form of overcoming the informational constraint. Our argument is similar to his.

8. The absence of any institutional screening mechanism (like training diplomas and degrees) of job seekers leads to this feature. The hirer has no certification mechanism to ensure that labor of a desired quality is hired. See Chapter 5 for discussion.

   See George Ackerlof "Market for 'Lemons,' Quality, Uncertainty and the Market Mechanism," *Quarterly Journal of Economics*, vol. 84 (Aug. 1970): 488–500. Unorganized labor markets would face adverse selection problems unless they report to informal contracts. Also see Yoram Barzel, "Fallacies of Information Costs," in *Journal of Law and Economics*, vol. 21 (September 1978), for related discussions.

9. C. C. von Weizsacker, *Barriers to Entry* (Berlin: Springer Verlager, 1980). Weizsacker explores barriers to entry in product markets in industrialized countries. Although the circumstances are very different in less-developed countries, the logic is similar in many product and factor markets.

10. These issues relating to the urban informal sector are discussed in Chapter 5.

11. See James M. Buchanan, Robert Tollison, and Gordon Tullock, *Toward a Theory of Rent Seeking Society* (College Station: Texas A & M Press, 1980), for an exploration of these views.
12. This theme is discussed in Chapter 4.
13. Formal organizations acquire importance in this analysis because several formal and semiformal institutions are being used in developing countries to foster economic development. The effectiveness of these organizations as delivery systems cannot be appreciated unless one is able to appreciate the types of informal contracting processes they generate.
14. See Furubotn, "Towards a General Theory of Property Rights," in Furubotn and Pejovich, *The Economics of Property Rights*.
15. N. S. Jodha, "Population Growth and the Decline of Common Property Resources in India," *Population and Development Review*, vol. 11, no. 2 (June 1985): 247–264.
16. R. D. Adgboye, "Land Tenures in Africa," in J. B. Wills and C. L. A. Leakey, eds., *Food Crops of the Low Land Tropics* (New York: Oxford University Press, 1977).
17. Garret Hardin, "The Tragedy of the Commons," reprinted in Ackerman, *Economic Analysis*.
18. When the legal system recognizes these intangible property rights (as in the case of purchased goodwill in the organized sector), exchange of such rights is possible. See Chapter 6 for discussion.
19. In the Coasian traditions, negative externalities arise because of costs associated with formal contracting processes (transactions costs).
20. See N. Vijay Jagannathan, *Conditions of Labor in the Bidi Industry of Murshidabad*, Department of Labour, Government of West Bengal (1974).
21. Jay O'Brien, "The Social Reproduction of Tenant Cultivation and Class Formation in the Gezira Scheme, Sudan," in *Review of Economic Anthropology*, A. Simon, ed. (Greenwich: Jay Publishing, 1984), pp. 218–241.
22. See Steven N. S. Cheung, "The Contractual Nature of the Firm," in *The Journal of Law and Economics,* vol. 26, no. 1 (April 1983): 1–23. In this article Cheung shows the remarkable manner in which transactions costs are minimized in Hong Kong despite widespread subcontracting.

4

Understanding Rural Contracts

This chapter offers a conceptual framework to analyze some existing and emerging contractual processes in labor and credit markets, which constitute important segments of the rural unorganized sector. For a large section of the work force in these markets, behavioral relations are utilized productively to secure earning opportunities.

Economic growth, most notably following the green revolution, has greatly increased the influence of markets and modern farming technology in rural areas of developing countries.[1] As a result of these factors, traditional rural communities have been opened up to the larger economic system. While the reciprocal nature of the village relationships has declined, new contractual arrangements have emerged based on evolving or existing conventions.

The analysis is conducted in four sections. The first section suggests some new dimensions to the concept of interlocked markets, an idea that has attracted considerable attention lately. The second section analyzes the role of a village in determining the nature and forms of rural contracts. The third section develops a model to explain how newly evolving conventions enable labor to secure tied rents in labor markets through general bilateral contracts. The final section discusses how rent-seeking behavior, together with general multilateral relations, is utilized to secure purchasing power in rural areas.

The Concept of Interlocked Markets

Studies of rural markets relations have shown that, despite several social and economic changes, the modern Indian village exhibits two interesting institutional characteristics.[2] First, markets for labor, land, and credit are closely interrelated in interlocked markets, where complex contractual relationships are established. Landowners secure regular and reliable labor supply from marginal cultivators and landless laborers, and in exchange meet the credit needs of these people.

Second, wage rates and interest rates vary not only between villages, but often even within villages. Remunerations appear to be determined by the terms and conditions laid out in informal contracts. Bardhan's study of village wage rates provides some convincing evidence to support this phenomenon in labor markets. His data for 3,500 agricultural workers in West Bengal has shown wide variations in village wage rates even in neighbouring areas, with the mean village wage being Rs. 2.76, with a standard deviation of Rs. 0.71. Further, these rates varied widely between the cultivating season and the lean season.[3]

The implications of these observations are quite profound for economic analysis. Market arrangements appear to be considerably more complex in unorganized markets than has been assumed by received theory, with informal contractual arrangements defining the penalty-reward system. Bardhan, Rudra, and several other economists have therefore argued for a comprehensive analytical approach to the land-labor-credit nexus in rural markets. This chapter hopes to provide some institutional perspectives to these market systems by laying out the microeconomic foundations of informal contracting processes.

Literature on interlocked markets, while recognizing the prevalence of informal contracts, has explained this phenomenon by suggesting that hirers are seeking to minimize production risks arising out of modern agricultural technology. The consequent labor market segmentation is therefore (implicitly) viewed as being caused by demand-induced factors.[4] The studies then suggest that these arrangements enable workers to secure employment from labor markets and simultaneously arrange with hirers for their consumption credit.

When wage advances are given by landowners, with a promise that the debtor repay as attached labor (with a daily wage) during the busy season, it is difficult to separate the loan component from wage payments. Workers view the whole compensation package as a means of resolving their cash-flow problems, so it is difficult to separate the earnings from the borrowings. Also, as Bardhan and Rudra's studies have revealed most advances do not carry a rate of interest.[5]

Such compensation packages are therefore, qualitatively different from (a) unsecured consumption credit that has an implicit interest rate (taken from village ration shops, tea shops, etc.), which seek to create purchasing power when earnings are inadequate to fulfill consumption needs, and (b) secured credit or credit in the conventional sense that is taken by providing tangible collateral to the creditors.

Perhaps a simpler way of understanding these exchanges is to view a person in a village as having one of the following informal contracting options:[6]

1. Wages can be secured from simple bilateral contracts in labor markets, where he or she sells time in the neoclassical sense, and specific behavioral relations with hirers are not worked out. This form corresponds to markets for daily-wage labor. A large segment of the labor force (particularly women and children) supplies such labor. Owing to considerable overpopulation, such wages are low, and increases in these wages in real terms have also not been particularly impressive.[7]

2. Apart from daily wages, labor can also secure tied rents in labor markets by investing in an appropriate behavioral contract through general bilateral relations. The hirers and the hired interact with each other at several levels of contact. Labor has an opportunity of earning these rents by offering a vector of attributes or "resources" desired by the hirers of services.

3. Workers could also acquire accretions of purchasing power as consumption credit because of some institutional characteristics of village communities. This type of credit, taken as unsecured consumption loans, helps bridging their earnings gap. The gap arises when earned income falls short of consumption requirements of the individuals. The interesting feature of such credit arrangements is the absence of any tangible surety or collateral available with the borrower.[8] The rationale behind such arrangements is analyzed in the concluding section of this chapter.

The three sources of earning capability lead one to question whether the terms "earnings" and "borrowings" used by economists like Bardhan and Rudra are appropriate categorizations in such markets. Instead, the poor can be considered to exercise options of selecting earning strategies from the three contracting alternatives described above in order to satisfy their consumption needs.

Instead of labor and credit markets being interlocked, earnings are postulated to be obtained through interlinked contracts that are secured in the factor markets. In labor markets, general bilateral relations generate these incomes. In credit markets, a complex system of interlinked contracts enables the poor to secure access to purchasing power.[9]

A combination of the three possibilities listed above determines the economic entitlements or earning capabilities of the rural poor. A combination of (1) and (2) creates social assets in labor markets, while (1) and (3) or (2) and (3) amount to interlinked contracts causing parallel property right formations.[10] The behavioral relations leading to these earning capabilities are nurtured and protected as property rights. The rural poor are thus able to use different forms of implicit contracts to create for themselves sets of informal property rights in village communities.

The next section examines the significant role villages play in shaping rural markets. As informal institutions villages (a) segment labor markets (thereby increasing the countervailing power of labor), and (b) provide a rationale for consumption credit for the rural poor.

The Village as an Unstructured Organization

The structure of rural contracting processes is influenced by the existence of village communities, because the latter provide several positive externalities during production and exchange. Lipton and Connell describe a village as having

> agricultural livelihood and production; geographical differentiation of habitation; geographical differentiation of rights in land; work places for most people within the same geographically differentiated boundaries as those of their habitation; small population size; a high proportion of internal transactions, and some degree of administrative differentiation.[11]

Two points from this extract are of particular interest to this chapter. These are: (a) villages have a high proportion of internal transactions, or what amounts to labor market segmentation; and (b) villages also exhibit a degree of administrative differentiation.

Role of Villages in Segmenting Labor Markets

As Dasgupta has shown in his analysis of village-based data collected from several studies in India, most villagers secure earning opportunities within their village.[12] The reasons for this are several—covering social, cultural, and economic factors. Some of the factors relevant for this analysis are briefly examined below.

Perhaps the most important economic factor is the high cost of information, arising out of the spatial dispersion of villages. Apart from poor transportation facilities, intervillage communications are generally unsatisfactory. By contrast, within villages a whole network of general multilateral relations results in great information externalities. Under these circumstances, the opportunity costs of acquiring information on the reliability or credit-worthiness of a worker from another village becomes relatively difficult, while the capabilities and attitudes of village workers are well known. From a hirer's perspective, contracting with village workers minimizes risks of qualitative uncertainty, and also assures stability of long-term relations.

In a study of a village in Maharashtra in India, Lee Schlesinger describes the nature of these bonds. For instance, when farmers have to prepare the land for cultivation they need additional help to handle heavy iron plows. Informal groups known as Payras are formed for sowing and planting. The members of a Payra (known as Payrakars) reciprocate help during the agricultural operations. The group normally retains its membership for a number of years. Obviously, such groups can succeed only if their members have sufficient mutual trust of each other, and have no fear of any single member taking a 'free ride' at others' expense.[13]

A second factor is the prevalence of intense poverty. For the very poor, informal groups based on kinship, tribes, or castes serve as institutions that alleviate the deprivations of poverty. They afford entertainment and opportunities for socializing even when earning opportunities are meager.[14] Frequent socialization and the reciprocal nature of relationships also serve the purpose of collectively providing insurance if one of the members is deprived of his or her earning source.

Village groups serve as important poverty-alleviating institutions. These socialization externalities imply that members are not likely to leave the village environment easily in search of alternate employment, a point that Schlesinger's study also confirms.

Social and cultural factors tend to reinforce these features People living in a village are bound together by social, religious, and economic events. There is a succession of festivals, natural disasters, marriages, births, and deaths that are participated in jointly. These factors together create a bond of belonging to a community.

Institutional Aspects of a Village

Apart from segmenting labor markets, a village also plays an important institutional role of serving as the basic administrative unit, a point that economists, unlike other social scientists have not adequately analyzed so far. In a study of lobby groups, Guttman, for instance, has demonstrated that villages as interest groups have successfully secured larger shares of developmental funds.[15] The point of interest is that developmental funds are usually allocated as grants for various facilities in the village such as schools, health centers, roads, drainage, and sanitation. In these situations, village characteristics can often play a critical role in determining allocations. For instance, a village with high landlessness can usually lay a much stronger claim for governmental programs and assistance.

If members of a village lobby collectively, they can greatly facilitate the inflow of governmental resources into their communities—resources that can later be reallocated (or misappropriated) among members of the community through informal contracts.[16] In addition, when public policy directly affects villagers (administrative inquiries on landholdings, repayment of governmental loans, misuse of ration cards, and procurement of food grain from affluent farmers), the collective silence of the village can be of immense benefit to individuals affected by the inquiry. While the affluent are able to acquire economic benefits from lobbying and rent seeking activities, the poor are able to utilize the mere fact that they belong to the village to acquire purchasing power, as a price in exchange for their silence during awkward administrative inquiries.

This line of argument holds true for villages where the number of peasant proprietors is fairly large. If, in addition, one recognizes inefficiencies of legal enforcement systems, discussed in chapter 2, landowners have another reason to maintain close relations with the poor in the village. Paradoxically, if class lines are clearly demarcated on the basis of property owned, or if affluent people in the village have strong connections in the administrative and political system, they may be able to directly appropriate the benefits of developmental funds without the need for any informal contracts with the poor.

Villages in developing countries are therefore hypothesized to be loose, informal organizations, where every member secures some form of administrative externalities by simply belonging to them.[17] The unstructured informal organization allows all villagers to acquire some contracting capabilities at home. This can be considered an important supply-side factor that builds up labor's countervailing power in rural markets.

The village as a loosely knit organization has within it coalitions of several smaller social groups, who utilize conventions and norms to contract using one of the options discussed: They can secure employment as daily wage labor in segmented labor markets; create for themselves social assets by engaging in longer (term) contracts; or obtain purchasing power in credit markets by simply belonging to the community.[18] The role of a village as an informal institution has to be recognized when analyzing rural contracting processes, particularly to understand the countervailing power of village labor.

The next two sections shows how the poor in villages of developing countries are able to utilize informal contracts in labor and credit markets, and secure for themselves fairly steady economic entitlements.

The Process of Informal Contracting in Rural Labor Markets

The causal factors of informal contracting processes have been discussed in Chapter 3. The compulsions of the new technology have made hirers interested in having stable long-term contracts with labor. In addition, the previous section has argued that the village as an informal organization segments labor markets. With these caveats, the actual contracting mechanism can be examined from the hired worker's perspective in order to understand (a) how labor is able to generate differential wages through behavioral relations or informal contracts, and (b) the opportunity costs of workers who agree to such contracts.

A hired worker has to decide on the level of general bilateral relations he would like to maintain with the hirer of labor services. His choices cover a range of relationships, from simple bilateral relations as a daily wage laborer-selling only time (as assumed by neoclassical theory)—to more complex relations, where general bilateral contracts are used to make him an attached worker. There are, in addition, several intermediate possibilities where he works as a semi-attached worker.

A Conceptual Framework

The forms of labor contracts can be explained by asking a simple question: What are the resources available for a landless agricultural worker in rural labor markets, and what can they be used to acquire?

One can hypothesize that labor has a choice between the following categories of activities in the labor market.

1. Generation of social assets or informal property rights. By an appropriate usage of resources a worker can generate a set of extra legal property rights through general bilateral relations with the hirer of labor services.
2. Participation in the daily wage-labor market by offering the services of just time, as assumed by standard neoclassical economics.
3. Use of all or part of the social assets that have been generated. Individuals can choose to develop their social assets partially, and continue to remain in the wage-labor market.

These activities are subject to some resource constraints. In neoclassical microeconomics, labor has only time to sell as a resource, and the worker's supply curve depends on his subjective allocation between labor and leisure. This analysis suggests, however, that even manual labor with no discernible skills has behavioral and physical attributes that can be sold as resources in labor markets.

In the model, "resource endowments" include not only the time dimension of neoclassical economics, but also several other resources or endowments a worker can utilize. Some of these resources are available as natural endowments, while others depend on the individual's subjective set of preferences. The resources used in generating social assets are categorized as time resource, behavioral resources, physical resource, locational resources, and the social assets themselves.

TIME RESOURCE

This is the most familiar resource in microeconomic models. Under conditions of intense poverty, while time may not have the same opportunity costs as in normal labor markets, it continues to remain a limited, exhaustible resource.

BEHAVIORAL RESOURCE

An individual's behavior at first glance does not appear to be a resource in the conventional sense of the term. In fact, economists usually describe the behavior of a person as arising from his subjective set of preferences. When, however, employment is secured in a highly personalized system, contact between the hirer and the hired is fundamentally different from the "assembly-line" situation. Contact requires a mode of behavior appropriate to the hirer's specifications.

Several additional attributes may be required from labor—such as reliability, trustworthiness, and flexibility. The first two acquire great significance in any informal relationship as there are no formal institutions for negotiating and enforcing contracts.

Cultural and social factors may increase the importance of the behavioral resource. For instance, a clear understanding of local mores, customs, and etiquette becomes an important prerequisite for hiring. Even within the same village there may be a clash of cultural values that makes conforming to a particular behavioral mode have significant opportunity costs (in an implicit sense).[19]

In these situations, a worker's set of preferences can determine his contracting capability. A docile, subservient, but physically strong person has much greater earning opportunities than an aggressive shirker! A person's subjective preference defines the amount of behavioral adjustment or attitudinal flexibility that is feasible. A worker desiring general bilateral relations has to weigh the pros and cons of conforming to the behavioral stipulations. He may, in fact, be willing to make only limited behavioral adaptations because the stipulations required by the hirer may involve high psychic or social costs.

For many workers, the behavioral resource available is circumscribed further if the person is forced to compromise accepted social and cultural norms of his caste, tribe, or kinship group—something costly in terms of cultural deprivation. Under these circumstances individuals may prefer maintaining general multilateral relations within their social group to developing general bilateral relations with landowners.[20] The conflict is resolved on a person-to-person level on the basis of individual preference functions. The behavioral endowments available for creating social assets through general bilateral relations will vary greatly across individual workers.

In the modern context there is another important dimension added to the behavioral resource. When labor is politicized, the behavioral resource becomes extremely important, because unionization of landless laborers makes landowners face a new set of management problems. They will be willing to offer rents for "well-behaved" workers, who can be expected to remain loyal to them during militant trade union activities. Again, as in the earlier example, workers have to make a hard choice: while some will perceive greater long-term benefits through unionization, others might prefer to build social assets. Individual preference functions will dictate how much of this resource the person is willing to use.[21]

PHYSICAL RESOURCE

Another separate resource is the physical resource supplied by the person. Agricultural operations in peasant farms of developing countries require short bursts of high effort level. Unlike the assembly lines of an industry, a number of critical emergencies arise because of the uncontrollable nature of farm environments. Unexpected rainfall, and attacks by pests and floods, are more like random variables for farmers, who require strong supportive help from workers at short notice. In normal years, the level of effort required may be much lower. In effect, labor may be required to perform a wide range of vaguely defined extra roles. These functions cannot be given specific payments, because their marginal contributions are impossible to predict or ascertain. Instead of drawing up an elaborate contract specifying the duties and obligations of both parties, it is much simpler to award labor with suitable rental share.

The physical resource depends on whether a person is capable of effort in the form of hard labor much above what is normally required. Obviously, physical strength will be the main factor determining this. With low nutritional levels, physical strength can always be expected to earn a premium in rural labor markets.

The physical resources at a person's disposal depend on his or her natural endowments, as well as subjective inclination or flexibility to use it. This inclination will dictate the laborer's sum total of behavioral and physical resources.[22]

The physical resource suggests that, despite modernization, muscle power retains its premium in farm employment. If all farming operations are automated in the Western model, labor will lose a considerable part of these rents.[23]

LOCATIONAL RESOURCE

Another important resource that earns rent arises from simply living in the village, an idea developed earlier. The value of this resource will vary from village to village, depending on the prevailing administrative and socialization externalities.[24] By remaining in a village—not leaving the physical or social space—a landless laborer may be able to secure some rent. Differential rents earned will depend on the specific power relations. This can explain why even between adjacent villages wage rates are rarely equal. In fact, one can make a testable proposition that wages will be higher in villages where all

individuals belong to a common sociocultural group such as a caste
or tribe.

Forms of Labor Contracts

The idea being developed here is simple: labor uses different amounts
of resources to earn varying amounts of tied rents. For instance, a
worker using his naturally endowed physical strength, plus having
total loyalty to the landowner, will be able to fully develop general
bilateral relations and maximize his social assets. At the other end of
the scale are the physically weak and the rebel, who have to be con-
tent with daily wage labor.[25]

ATTACHED LABOR (BEHAVIORAL + PHYSICAL + LOCATIONAL)

This combination leads to attached labor. The worker is like a full-
time servant, very often living on the landowner's property. His income level is substantially above that of the landless. In a computa-
tion the author had made in 1976 in Burdwan district (West Bengal,
India), attached labor was securing twice the income of the landless
on an annual basis. Bardhan and Rudra's studies also indicate the
annual earnings of attached labor are substantially higher than daily
labor.[26]

SEMIATTACHED LABOR

If a worker is either unwilling to devote enough of, say, the behavioral resource, or simply lacks the required physical resources, he
falls into one of the categories of semiattached labor. As Bardhan
and Rudra have shown, there are several forms of semiattached labor.

1. *Physical + Locational:* As long as technology in developing countries retains its bias toward land-intensive cultivation by improving the genetic quality of plants, muscle power or physical
   strength can be reasonably expected to earn rents in a village.
   With widespread poverty and deprivation, many are not able
   to reach their potential physical strength. A person endowed
   with muscle power can secure rents from landowners, even if
   he is not willing to compromise on behavioral factors. Such
   workers would typically be given short-term contracts for the
   duration of the cultivation season or for specific jobs, and can
   be described as one of the categories of semiattached labor.
2. *Behavioral + Locational:* Such a person can be expected to earn
   less rent than a person contracting physical endowments. But

the behavioral factor gains in importance with unionization of agricultural labor, or during agrarian unrest. This combination leads to another variation of semiattached labor.

DAILY-WAGE LABOR

Locational: By itself, being an "insider" would not generate much rent, but this factor can explain differences in wages between adjoining villages observed in empirical studies. Landowners may pay the wage differentials, depending on their valuation of the importance of fellow villagers.

In conclusion, labor is able to earn differential wages by negotiating contracts using different endowments of resources. These arrangements could explain why wage remunerations in the rural sector for labor exhibit wide diversity, while theories based on western paradigms predict low subsistence wages.[27]

Implications for Institutional Economics

Institutional economists have addressed themselves only to labor market conditions in industrialized countries. Their analysis has indicated how formal organizations like firms have emerged to resolve several monitoring and transactions costs problems in labor and product markets. What this analysis has sought to demonstrate is that endogenous informal contracting processes not only enable individuals to pool their risks, but also provide several positive externalities. Labor, even under conditions of intense poverty, has options of utilizing behavioral relations productively and securing earning differentials by providing miscellaneous work of desired quality or reliability.[28] Behavioral relations therefore have a productive aspect worth examining.

The second theme that needs to be further examined is how the village as an unstructured organization increases the contracting options of unattached labor to secure earning capabilities.

Informal Contracts in Credit Markets

Opportunity Costs of Extending Credit to the Poor

The last section analyzed the methods by which labor is able to generate rents or differential wages in labor markets. A substantial proportion of the labor force may either be unwilling to sacrifice behavioral resources or simply lack the physical resources needed to earn these rents. For such people, income earned is restricted to a few months in the cultivating season, leading to an "earnings gap." Credit requirements consequently become a recurring feature for satisfying basic consumption needs for food, clothing, medicine, and entertainment.[29] These workers also obviously lack tangible property rights.

When labor receives unsecured consumption credit as accretions to purchasing power, lenders cannot be expected to make the usual economic calculation of expecting a fair return on investment. They are providing these agricultural laborers with credit on the basis of virtually no collateral in the conventional sense. Given the level of poverty found in South Asian countries, even if usurious interest rates are charged, borrowers have no means of repaying these consumptions loans. So monetary return for capital invested in this manner is likely to be extremely low; especially when one considers the long list of institutions trying to mobilize rural savings (ranging from banks and credit cooperatives to small savings organizations and rural post offices).[30]

The standard justification given for the lender's behavior centers around an economic and a sociological argument. The economic explanation has sought to explain the phenomenon by suggesting a land-labor-credit nexus.

The preceding analysis, however, argued that (a) wage advances given to contracted labor are qualitatively different from consumption credit, and (b) a substantial section of the labor force in villages still earns its livelihood in the daily wage market, where contracts involve the standard neoclassical form of simple bilateral relations. There has to be a reason why the affluent are willing to offer credit to such persons who are either unwilling or unable to create social assets through general bilateral contracts.

The sociological argument explaining rural consumption credit suggests the prevalence of tradition—based conventions in villages, with norms defining rights and obligations of all members. As was discussed earlier, with the growth of markets and modernization, most of these social norms have been disappearing rapidly because affluent villagers have begun neglecting their hierarchical obligations.

Interlinked Contracts in Credit Markets

An alternate explanation for the prevalence of rural credit markets for the very poor rests on two propositions: (a) Information and administrative externalities these poor individuals possess by remaining in a village allow them some contracting capabilities; and (b) the presence of general multilateral relations within such groups reduces freerider problems, thereby decreasing lenders' risks in contracting with such persons. Because of these two factors, creditors are able to interlink contracts with the poor and generate for themselves simultaneously a set of parallel property rights.

Credit arrangements are worked out, with the poor surrendering their future property rights from governmental programs to the creditors. The behavioral relations among the debtors are used as a substitute for tangible surety or collateral.

As discussed previously, with the exposure of villages to a few decades of developmental administration, there is always an expectation that governmental schemes and programs will be implemented in the villages.[31] These programs may be either specific to the village or, more likely, for a target group (consisting of, say, individuals below the poverty level across villages). In both cases, however, informal contracting arrangements among villagers can be used to divert monetary and material benefits to the affluent members of the community.

In these programs, such as providing relief work or distributing sugar, cooking fuel, and wheat, the actual amount of largess reaching a recipient is a very small proportion of his family's requirements. Alternately, the goods being distributed may not rank high on his list of preferences. At the individual level the property rights generated by these measures are not sufficient to permanently close the earnings gap. At a collective level, however, these do represent sizable, recurring grants or subsidized goods to village communities. So shopkeepers and landowners (the few) enter into informal arrangements with the landless (the many), by which the latter do not challenge the appropriation of developmental funds and material intended for them, and instead receive as a quid-pro-quo consumption loans during the lean season.

One can speculate that a consequence of these contracts is that the implicit interest rates charged on consumption of loans fluctuate widely, depending on prevailing power equations in a village. If the affluent villagers have powerful connections in the administration, the need for maintaining such contracts is automatically reduced.

The landless are therefore afforded credit facilities in return for mortgaging their current and future property rights given by the government. Although landowners may have high opportunity costs when one just looks at the capital market, the picture becomes radically different when other institutional factors are introduced.

While governmental programs provide the rationale for such contracts, the real significance lies in the manner in which enforceability is ensured. As in all situations where groups of individuals collectively contract, free riders (in this case squealers) can normally be expected to make such contracts unenforceable.[32] This is where general multilateral relations among the poor play an important role. Whenever administrative inquiries are made by officials on the misuse of welfare funds, inquiring officials usually experience a collective silence from the affected poor even where political awareness is high. No one will volunteer information about the misuse of public funds because as a group they consider their relations with affluent villagers more enduring than any short-term gain from exposing the guilty parties. A set of conventions within a group is therefore effectively used to generate earning opportunities in the village.[33]

This section is concluded with a brief illustration from West Bengal, India, to show the significance of informal contractual relations for consumption credit.

About three decades ago, the Government of India established an industrial city at Durgapur in West Bengal with an investment of about $1 billion. As most jobs in the organized industrial sector in the new city required at least a high school diploma, the major beneficiaries of the job openings from the surrounding villages were affluent landowners who already had the necessary educational prerequisites. The following chain of events resulted:

1. Landowners in villages with good communications with the city continued to reside in their villages, but began to neglect agricultural operations.
2. The landless found credit conditions extremely tight because village landowners who had obtained factory jobs preferred to invest their savings in banks and savings institutions. By 1976 Durgapur had the highest small savings deposit rate in India.
3. There was a qualitative change in public lobbying for developmental funds within a village. The greatest pressure was for better transport links (mainly bus services with Durgapur city).
4. Economic entitlements collapsed for the very poor—leading to arson, terrorism, and murder.[34]

Conclusion

Rural contracts relations can be characterized by two sets of relations. First, in labor markets workers and hirers of labor services engage in hierarchical relations through which different levels of wages can be earned. Second, individuals, by interacting together in informal groups, are able to secure additions to their earnings by using behavioral relations to acquire contracting capabilities. They use these institutional devices to mortgage property rights made available through governmental programs. In both cases, intangible behavioral relations define sets of economic entitlements for the poor. These property rights enable individuals to survive and participate in the village society. The rights also determine who will move to the city and who will not.

Notes and References

1. See Keith Griffin, "Growth and Impoverishment in Rural Areas of Asia," *World Development*, vol. 7, nos. 4/5 (April/May 1979): 361–384. Also Keith Griffin and A. R. Khan, "Poverty in the Third World: Ugly Facts and Fancy Models," in *World Development*, vol. 6, no. 3 (March 1978): 295–304. Also Yujiro Hayami and Masao Kikuchi, *Asian Village Economy at the Crossroads* (Baltimore: University of Tokyo Press and Johns Hopkins University Press, 1982).
2. The best-known studies are by Pranab Bardhan and Ashok Rudra. See Ashok Rudra, *Indian Agricultural Economics: Some Myths and Realities* (New Delhi: Allied Publishers, 1982). Also Pranab Bardhan and Ashok Rudra, "Terms and Conditions of Labour Contracts in Agriculture: Result of a Survey in West Bengal 1979," in *Oxford Bulletin of Economics and Statistics*, vol. 43, no. 1 (Feb., 1983): 89–111. A survey of the literature has been conducted by Pranab Bardhan. See Bardhan, "Interlocking Factor Market and Agrarian Development: A Review of Issues," in *Oxford Economic Papers,* vol. 32 (1980): 82–90. A theoretical analysis based on National Sample: Survey Data for Eastern India has been conducted by Pranab Bardhan, "Wages and Unemployment in a Poor Agrarian Economy: A Theoretical and Empirical Analysis" in *Journal of Political Economy*, vol. 87, no. 3, (1978): 497–500. Also Sheila Bhalla, "New Relations of Production in Haryana Agriculture," *Economic and Political Weekly* (March 1976). As the author has primary experience in the same area studied by Bardhan and Rudra, their findings are used extensively to support the arguments in this chapter.
3. See Bardhan, "Wages and Unemployment."
4. See Mukesh Eswaran and Ashol Kotwal, "A Theory of Two-Tier Labor Markets in Agrarian Economies," *American Economic Review*, vol. 75, no. 1 (1985): 162–177. In the article the authors mention some supply-side considerations such as risk aversion among workers who would prefer the stability of long-term contracts to the uncertainties of spot markets. An additional supply-side factor which should be considered is the role of a village in (a) segmenting labor markets and (b) providing other contracting options to labor.

5. In fact, a wage advance is akin to an employee's taking an advance from his provident funds or some other personal savings, a very common feature in public and private institutions in the organized sector. Of course, if the wage advance carries an implicit interest rate, the argument loses its force.

6. Poverty has several manifestations, but two are of particular significance for this analysis. First, individuals are unable to secure enough food to fulfill their basic energy requirements, leading to a calorie gap. John W. Mellor and Bruce F. Johnston in their article, "The World Food Equation," in the *Journal of Economic Literature,* vol. 22, no. 2, (June 1984): 531–574, quote Reutlinger's study for the mid-sixties indicating that 1.1 billion people in the world were on a calorie-deficient diet. Second, these people lack the purchasing power to buy consumer goods, entertainment, and liquor from the market system.

7. See Gustav F. Papanek, "Real Wages, Growth, Inflation, Income Distribution and Politics in Pakistan, India, Bangladesh, Indonesia." Discussion Paper No. 29 (Boston University, Economics Department, 1979).

8. In fact, both the borrower and the lender are often aware that there is only a remote possibility of repayment of the loan.

9. Land has been deliberately excluded from this analysis because informal contracts leading to tenancy are basically derived property rights. This study has been restricted to original, intangible property rights. See Chapters 2 and 3 for discussion.

10. Bardhan and Rudra distinguish at least five types of contractual relationships at the village. These are: (a) fully attached labor; (b) semi-attached labor, ranging from labor attached for a particular season or period, to labor attached on a more casual basis (where laborers are allowed to contract with other hirers as well), and labor that is available at beck and call; and (c) fully unattached labor, corresponding to the neoclassical labor markets. Our analysis will show how each of these forms arises from different combinations of wages and rent in labor markets. See Bardhan and Rudra in *Oxford Bulletin* (note 2).

11. John Connell and Michael Lipton, *Assessing Village Labour Situations* (New York: Oxford University Press, 1977). The quotation is from p. 12.

12. Biplab Dasgupta, with Roy Laishley, Henry Lucas, and Brian Mitchell, *Village Society and Labour Use* (New York: Oxford University Press, 1977). Also David G. Mandelbaum, *Society in India, Change and Continuity* (Los Angeles: University of California Press, 1970). For Africa, see David J. Parkin, *Palms, Wine and Witnesses* (San Francisco: Chandler Publishing Co., 1972). Also Hayami and Kikuchi, "Asian Village Economy."

13. Lee I. Schlesinger, "Agriculture and Community in Apshinge in Satara District, Maharashtra," in *Research in Economic Anthropology,* vol. 4, George Dalton, ed. (New York: Jai Press, 1981).

14. Some of the most vigorous forms of folk dance and music in rural India are performed by tribal and scheduled caste communities, and invariably involve collective effort. Poverty in a village does not deprive a person of a varied social and cultural life.

15. Joel M. Guttman, "Villages as Interest Groups: Demand for Agricultural Extension Services in India," *Kyklos,* vol. 33, fasc. 1 (1980): 122–141.

16. This rent-seeking aspect has interesting implications for rural contracting processes and could provide an additional reason for the observed isolationist or segmented nature of rural labor markets.

17. The argument put forward here has some parallels with Williamson's description of formal organizations in *Markets and Hierarchies* (New York: Free Press, 1975). While Williamson argues that negative externalities force markets to be replaced by hierarchies, in these examples positive externalities result in villages acquiring characteristics of informal organizations, and providing preferential access to local villagers.

18. Labor market conditions can therefore vary in tightness, even with overpopulation. Labor from outside the village often finds employment, too, but usually with fewer privileges, particularly for unsecured credit.

19. For instance, the worker may belong to a community where drinking liquor is an essential part of social life. The hirer can, on the other hand, for cultural and social reasons insist on total abstinence, even when labor is not actually working in his field. To give another example, the landowner may consider eating pork or beef "unclean," although the worker's religiocultural beliefs permit him to do so. Clashes of cultural values become acute when landowners and the landless belong to different religious communities.

20. These situations involve a clash of two poverty-alleviating institutions— long-term contracts with landowners secure regular income streams, while socializing in the informal group improves the quality of life even without any money!

21. An interesting implication is that trade union activities among landless laborers convey benefits to the entire group of agricultural workers.

22. Harvey Liebenstein's X-efficiency concept can be explained in terms of behavioral and physical resources individuals are investing in work. These resources create endogenous conventions that guarantee the effort levels of workers. See Harvey Liebenstein, "X Efficiency." Also see Louis De Alessi, "Property Rights Transactions Costs and X-Efficiency," in *American Economic Review*, vol. 73, no. 1 (March 1983): 64–81.

23. Some interesting perspectives can be found in Murray J. Leaf, "The Green Revolution and Cultural Change in a Punjab Village, 1965–1978," *Economic Development and Cultural Change*, vol. 31, no. 2 (Jan. 1983): 227– 270. Also, "The Green Revolution Revisited," by George Blyn, in *Economic Development and Cultural Change*, vol. 31, no. 4 (July 1983): 705– 726. Also see Bhalla and Chadha, "Green Revolution and the Small Peasant."

24. The locational factor implies that even for landless labor there could be opportunity costs of migrating to cities, a theme developed in Chapter 7.

25. Forms of contracts are assumed to be one of the categories discussed by Bardhan and Rudra (note 2).

26. Such persons tend to be very loyal to their masters during inspections and inquiries by government officials. They are able to secure a "trickle down" of benefits from landowners as a reward for loyalty.

27. Even if semiattached labor receives wages higher than its marginal product during lean seasons (as wage advances), and less than its marginal

product during the attached period (busy season), the total earnings are likely to be more than for unattached labor. This is confirmed by the Bardhan and Rudra study.

28. Such earnings can be described as rent because it is impossible to impute values to these remunerations on a graded scale.

29. It should be noted that the credit being discussed in this section is unsecured consumption credit to the very poor and not production credit. They comprise daily laborers and many of the contracted workers without any tangible property rights. Lenders' risks here will be very different when compared with secured loans. Usury in these two cases is obviously qualitatively different.

30. This distinction has not been made in some of the well-known studies. See Amit Bhadhuri, "On Formation of Usurious Interest Rates in Backward Agriculture," *Cambridge Journal of Economics,* vol. 1 (1977): 341–352. Also Kaushik Basu, "Implicit Interest Rate, Usury and Isolation in Backward Agriculture," *Cambridge Journal of Economics,* vol. 8, no. 2 (June 1984: 145–160). These analyses do not explain credit given to the very poor as accretions of purchasing power during the lean season when the lender is aware that the debtor lacks repayment capabilities in a conventional sense.

31. For a study of the working of development administration, see Ronald J. Herring and Rex. J. Edwards, "Guaranteeing Employment to the Rural Poor: Social Functions and Class Interests in the Employment Guarantee Scheme in Western India," *World Development,* vol. 11, no. 7 (1983): 575–592. Also see Michael Lipton, "Agricultural Finance and Rural Credit in Poor Countries," *World Development,* vol. 4, no. 7 (1976): 543–553.

32. Unenforceability of such contracts means breaking the collective silence during administrative inquiries.

33. This feature has been used to develop group-based credit programs. In India group-based savings and credit programs are being practiced by a large number of financial agencies. For a summary of experience, see B. M. Desai and B. L. Tripathi, *Group Based Savings and Credit Programmes in Rural India,* paper presented at the ILO Workshop on Group Based Savings and Credit Programmes, Bogra, Oct. 1983. The Bangladesh Grameen Bank has launched an innovative program using groups as collateral substitutes.

34. See Jagannathan, report, *Effects of Urbanization on Durgapur's Hinterland and the Jangal Mahals: A Socio-Economic Survey.*

5

A Taxonomy of
the Urban Informal Sector

Urbanization in developing countries has been accompanied by many glaring manifestations of poverty. Notable among them is widespread business activity in unorganized urban markets or, to use a popular expression, the *urban informal sector*. In this sector, as in its rural counterpart, contracts are negotiated and executed outside the formal legal system. This chapter gives a taxonomy of the urban informal sector, explaining how—as in rural areas—behavioral relations are utilized to generate wealth during production and exchange.

The concepts developed are based on available empirical evidence. Since the 1970s a wealth of empirical studies have been conducted on the dynamics of economic activities in the urban informal sector, and on forms of labor markets generated, as well as several other facets of urban poverty.[1]

These studies have demonstrated that the urban informal sector consists of a wide variety of urban occupations in developing countries. Some of the vocations are highly competitive service activities in the tertiary or service sector, ranging from teashops to garbage collection, from street entertainers to shoeshine boys, where sellers deal directly with buyers of services. As start-up costs and profit margins are low, these occupations rarely have markets for hired labor. Others cover more complex organizations such as small-scale manufacturers, repair workers, and cheap restaurants, where the need for division of labor leads to the hiring of wage labor.

The informal sector can be characterized as having two forms of employment systems. In marginal service activities and microproduction units, individuals are mostly self-employed and work in highly competitive market environments. In larger units requiring some technology or management, unorganized labor markets exist. The ILO definition of the urban informal sector takes both these perspectives into account. It states:

> It (the informal sector) consists of small scale units engaged in production and distribution of goods and services with the primary objective of generating employment and incomes to their participants notwithstanding the constraints on capital, both physical and human, and knowhow.[2]

This chapter explains the workings of the urban informal sector using the framework of extralegal property rights developed so far. The first section provides continuity from the last chapter by highlighting the differences in institutional features between rural and urban unorganized markets. In the second section, an illustrative model is developed to outline methods by which general multilateral contracts are utilized for appropriating locational rents in urban areas. The third section suggests how behavioral relations are productively utilized in informal markets for hired labor in cities. The final section examines whether the informal sector has the potential of being used as a vehicle to promote economic growth.

Institutional Features of the Urban Informal Sector

Similarities with the Rural Sector

A common strand connecting the unorganized markets in urban and rural areas is that most social institutions in the former are direct extensions of the latter.[3] Empirical studies have consistently indicated the strong social and cultural affinities members of the urban informal sector retain with villages or regions of origin. Rural social groupings such as tribes, castes, and clans serve a social role in the impersonal urban environment. In a study of a Bombay slum, Owen Lynch has described the important role the feeling of cultural identity plays among the slum dwellers. Facing an impersonal and hostile civic environment, particularly abysmal sanitation, lack of privacy, and inadequate shelter, an identity on the basis of linguistic, caste, and religious ties, provides some salve for the ego.[4] Kin-based and caste-based groups allow important socialization externalities for the urban poor.

Apart from this, groups also secure access to wealth collectively by (a) providing a method of nurturing and protecting extralegal property rights on locational rents, and (b) controlling access to employment opportunities during job hiring processes. In both these situations informal groups utilize existing conventions to restrict access to economic opportunities, earning rents in the process. The urban informal sector, like the rural sector therefore, faces market segmentation, and offers rent-seeking opportunities.

Differences with Rural Sector

There are, however, significant differences between the rural and urban unorganized markets that make a study of the urban informal sector important by itself. These rural-urban differences are:

1. Economic activities by individuals or groups in the urban informal sector operate in physical and working environments considerably more hostile than those in rural areas.

   There is no umbrella institution like the village affording all members privileges of countervailing power. The administrative machinery in cities is geared primarily toward the civic needs of the organized sector, and not the welfare needs of the poor. The informal sector, at best, is viewed as serving a peripheral role of urban economic life, and so contracting possibilities for consumption credit become limited.[5]

   The physical environment of squatter settlements, where the poor have to find shelter is invariably unhealthy with poor drainage, inadequate sanitation, and uncertain water supply. The high density of population and widespread prevalence of crime compound these problems.

   Working environments are equally harsh. Many of these activities flout some civic or labor law. Unlike rural activities, which are simply extralegal, these urban activities have in addition some illegal elements, leading to constant harassment from civic and police authorities.[6]

2. Informal contracting processes are also considerably greater in both numbers and complexity, reflecting the diverse nature of opportunities to earn a living in a city.

   Many activities have close links with production and consumption in the organized sector. For instance, a group may control access to some recyclable wastes. Alternatively, a vegetable vendor may be selling his products to a set of impersonal urban consumers. These are examples where microunits of self-employed persons interact directly with the formal sector. In other cases, the production units may be larger, and actually operate as subcontractors of the organized sector. These enterprises are likely to utilize the services of hired labor.

   A considerable range of activities is also generated within the informal sector without many linkages with the organized sector. These meet endogenous service requirements of consumption, housing, and credit. Obviously, the larger the informal sector, the greater will be the requirements of housing, food, and entertainment for its members, so diverse business opportunities arise within the sector when a city expands.

3. A third major difference is that in urban areas locational considerations are of great significance. Market demands for goods and services in urban areas have different densities across sections of geographic space. Even when explicit demand is not present, there could be potential markets at specific locations waiting to be tapped by an entrepreneur. For example, on a hot day a potential market exists for selling lemonade at a frequently used bus stand. Start-up cost of this activity is obviously low, and if in addition opportunity cost of supplying these services is low enough, as in developing countries, such a vocation will become attractive.[7] Because of the lack of adequate earning capabilities, such low-investment activities become profitable. A multitude of small and marginal establishments spring up near heavily populated public places such as government offices, railway stations, major shopping areas, and industrial estates, mainly to appropriate and monopolize available locational rents. The rapidity of business turnover in these activities contrasts sharply with the relatively slow pace of economic life in rural markets.

The urban picture, therefore, does indicate significant differences, in economic organization, and can be analyzed in two stages. First, how are behavioral relations utilized as a part of a production technique to secure and appropriate locational rents in densely populated sections of the city? To answer this question one has to show that when informal groups are able to control access to locations, they can perform a role analogous to that of the village discussed in Chapter 3 by segmenting markets. A simple illustrative model is developed in the next section to show the logic of these contracting arrangements. Second, within urban informal markets one can look at the nature of interlinked contractual relations. The ideas can then be used to assess the prospects of the urban informal sector.

Informal Groups and Locational Rents: A Model of Territorial Control

When population density is very high, as in large cities of developing countries, potential markets exist in a large number of activities. These sources of livelihood can be tapped if suitable methods can be devised to prevent excessive competition. For this a person or group of individuals must gain exclusive access to locational rents. Social groups can utilize a set of existing conventions to informally contract with each other, and collectively maintain control over such geographic areas. Critical to the process is the formulation of a "defense technology," which can preserve territorial control with or without any assistance from the legal system. This idea is explained below with the help of an illustrative model.

The Assumptions

The following assumptions are made to simplify the analysis:

1. The activity considered is an extremely simple one like selling peanuts. Potential demand for the product is uniformly distributed along a given urban space.
2. The peanut seller is a price taker. This is because the seller cannot control the competitive price for peanuts. If the seller tries to overprice the good, the buyer will reject the offer and locate another seller in close proximity. Alternatively, the buyer may simply decide to postpone his demand for peanuts if he considers them to be overpriced.

   The buyer's decision-making process is influenced by a very low-level equilibrium between search costs and search benefits. As net benefits of searching for peanuts are extremely low, there is not much incentive to search for the best price unless the peanut seller increases his price exorbitantly. In this sense this model of entry barrier is different from traditional models: even if a seller is able to erect a barrier he continues to remain a price taker.
3. Labor is the only factor of production. Selling peanuts requires very little investment except perhaps a movable stand. Requirements of credit are also low. In fact the only requirement is long hours of presence at the site.
4. Following from (3), as labor is the only factor of production, cost of production in the usual sense of the term is insignificant. Cost is mainly in the nature of expense incurred in acquiring the input (peanuts). For simplicity, these costs are assumed to be a constant proportion of total sales. Apart from this, the seller has to incur costs in excluding intruders from the market. These costs are hypothesized to be significant.
5. The peanut seller is too poor to employ material aids (like advertising) in order to increase sales. Perhaps the only way he

can increase sales is by decorating his stall or shouting to attract attention.

6. To begin with, one peanut seller controls the entire space. Whenever potential demand exists some people have to take on the role of entrepreneurs, to discover and exploit it. To begin with, assume that one such person has acted as the entrepreneur and set up the peanut stall, and the entire space or territory is controlled by him.

7. Although the seller controls the urban space, he has no legal right to do so.

Sales and Territory

If a peanut seller has a monopoly over his territory, he can be expected to maximize sale over the area. There is however one problem that has to be resolved. As the activity requires the seller's physical presence at one spot, potential demand that is located further away from his stall becomes more difficult to exploit. .This factor is likely to attract more peanut sellers, who will become potential rivals.

A major element of cost becomes the effort that has to be expended simply to prevent a given territory on turf from being encroached upon. The seller's opportunity cost is the level of effort or energy that has to be spent simply to maintain his turf. As a rational individual he can be expected to take measures to minimize his "defense" costs by reducing the level of effort that he has to expend. A convenient solution is to use informal contracts with others by which the group mutually agrees to keep others out (analogous to the cocoa companies described in Chapter 1).

Informal contracts with other established vendors, preferably in a complementary trade, or even in the same trade but operating from a different location, become a convenient solution. Very often local police and civic officials also offer these services on the payment of protection money.[8] An intruder therefore has to reckon with not only the existing seller's wrath, but also retributive actions from the group with whom the seller has informally contracted "defense arrangements." (See Appendix A for the formal model).

Two simple propositions follow from this. First, in public areas of high population density, the peanut seller and other hawkers will be united as a group to collectively guard their extralegal rights, while individuals control smaller but more paying sections of turf and privately appropriate locational rents. Even a simple betel nut seller in Calcutta's business district values his turf around $7,000. Second, as such informal contracts are easier to work out among groups having common social and cultural backgrounds, because free-rider problems may often arise when strangers contract with each other, ethnic homogeneity in trades and vocations becomes a commonly observed feature, as individuals belonging to common social groups are less likely to be opportunistic.

Through informal contracts peanut sellers may be able to effectively generate for themselves extralegal property rights, even on public property. These contracts create restrictions within the informal sector, and prevent universal access to earning opportunities.

An alternate assumption could be that the state or civic authorities recognize these rights, and give vendors licenses to operate from particular areas. It can be shown that even with a licensing system, the peanut sellers may prefer to utilize contracting mechanisms if they are unsure of prompt remedial action by the state authorities on an infringement of their rights. (See Appendix A).

Implications

The interesting feature of these contracting arrangements is that free-rider problems are not likely to emerge because of the nature of the informal contracts. These arrangements are used as a substitute for law, and participants are aware that a breach in contracts will lead not only to confusion—but of more importance—to a disappearance of the earning opportunity.

What follows is that entry into these informal sector activities is predictably, highly selective, causing different degrees of segmentation in markets. Another significant implication is that by using such methods groups can exploit almost any perceived rent-seeking opportunity in the city. The central business district experiences severe encroachment problems on public sidewalks and paths. The ILO studies have confirmed these features in all metropolitan areas of developing countries.

It is also easy to see how social groups may sometimes reach a collective agreement to hire the help of a professional "tough" in order to ensure exclusive control over paying urban locations. Criminal groups are thus prevalent in most such cities to provide such a role.

Turning back to the peanut seller, as the city begins to expand, the value of locations begins to increase. With the growth in sales, additional help is often required. In these activities, trust has to be given a high premium because a hired helper quickly learns the trade, and there is always a danger that he may decide to set up his own independent stall quickly, and become a rival. A more practical alternative is to induct a member of the immediate family or kinship group to share the work, so that existing social conventions can check opportunism. If sales continue to expand, the assistant may even be allowed to set himself up independently. Work sharing becomes a predictable feature of this model.[10] The effects on rural-urban migration would be significant, and are examined in Chapter 7.

Some Evidence to Support the Peanut Seller Model

The type of evidence required to confirm the model suggested above is available from studies made by urban anthropologists. To illustrate the scope of this model, some evidence is presented from Seoul (South Korea), Calcutta (India), Ibadan (Nigeria), and Mexico City (Mexico).

THE SHOESHINE GANGS OF SEOUL

The shoeshine gangs of Seoul, according to a study by Kang and Kang, are a part of a crime syndicate controlling a whole range of informal sector activities in the crowded sections of metropolitan Seoul.[11] Corresponding to the peanut seller in our model, but considerably more affluent is the Oaji (who 'owns' the territory). Oajis work in collusion with one another, and have their disputes settled by the Wang Cho or Head of the Gangsters. Within their territory they run shoeshine operations, tearooms, prostitution rings, and boarding houses. The Kang study concentrates only on the shoeshine boys and describes how Oajis exercise control and supervision over their "hired" labor. If any stranger tried to encroach on the territory, violence or threat of violence is used.

THE WASTE RECYCLERS OF CALCUTTA

Unlike the shoeshine operation, the waste recyclers of Calcutta control territory that does not easily attract the public eye, but plays a distinctly productive role.[12] According to Mitra, a large tract of marshy land to the east of Calcutta, which is used as waste disposal sites of the city, is controlled and put to productive use by about 100,000 individuals. These persons use endogenous institutions (caste and tribal groupings) to process whatever waste is recyclable. The activities carried out are very large in number, ranging from growing vegetables for the city (raised on organically manured soil) or picking and sorting of garbage, to tanning skins and hides and retrieving animal products for use in a variety of industrial goods. The many separate groups are able to maintain control informally over their territory through their caste-based conventions. Clearly, behavioral relations are being used productively.

THE BEGGARS OF IBADAN

The third example of territorial control is from Southern Nigeria in the city of Ibadan.[13] Bamisaiye describes how begging in the city of Ibadan is a Hausa monopoly, with the allocation of territory clearly demarcated by tribal chiefs. Except for blind beggars, who are itinerant, other beggars have allocated sites from which they operate. The profitability of the vocation is indicative of the fact that their average earnings were equal to that of unskilled labor, while some of the beggars interviewed had earned enough to make plans for starting private businesses.

A SLUM BLACK MARKET IN MEXICO CITY

This article in the *Wall Street Journal* again indicated the range of informal sector vocations in crowded parts of a city.[14] The Slum Black Market described in the report represents one of the largest informal markets in Mexico City and is located in a quarter-mile stretch of a busy street. About 180 vendors jam this street with a wide range of smuggled consumer goods. The business entrepreneurs include a large proportion of individuals who have some criminal backgrounds, Territoriality is maintained through informal contracting, and by using the services of professional toughs. Interestingly, the article mentions that the "most powerful leader" is a former professional boxer. A large number of small business enterprises have also arisen in the periphery, to take advantage of the large volume of shoppers passing through their turf, en route to the slum black market.

Discussion

Of the four examples given, two were perhaps in the nature of unproductive restrictions (Seoul and Mexico City), where corruption and extortion were inextricably linked with territorial control. The illustration from Calcutta involved behavioral relations being put to productive use by helping recycle urban wastes. The example from Ibadan was one of exploiting rent-seeking opportunities.

The purpose of the illustrations is not to pass normative judgments on which of the restriction-seeking activities are productive. Instead, it is hoped that these few illustrations will help the reader grasp the nature of income-generating capabilities in the urban informal sector. Such activities provide many civic services such as waste and refuse disposal, repair and maintenance work, transportation, and sometimes even domestic fuel in cities of developing countries. The useful lesson the examples reveal is the power of established conventions to appropriate income from economic opportunities. The Oajis of Seoul, the waste recyclers of Calcutta, and the beggars of Ibadan all utilized existing clan, caste, or tribal conventions to capture rent-seeking opportunities.

Other Forms of Behavioral Relations

The model discussed in the last section dealt with one facet of the informal sector: how informal contracts secure and appropriate locational rents in urban areas. In this section, markets within the informal sector are examined. These include markets for consumer goods (which, being similar to the peanut seller model, do not require separate analysis) and markets for labor, credit, and housing. To begin with, one can analyze contractual relations in labor markets, and later briefly explore contracting in housing and credit markets.

Urban Informal Labor Markets

Labor markets in the informal sector share the common feature of segmentation with their rural counterparts, although the causes are different. Mazumdar has analyzed and discussed these factors for data from India and Malaysia.[15] John Hariss, in a study of labor markets in Coimbatore (India), has shown how agricultural landowning castes segment access to the city's industrial work force, while landless laborers who (belong to the scheduled castes), have access mainly to casual daily wage labor.[16] Similar studies are available for a large number of developing countries, indicating that labor markets are highly segmented, with access restricted to individuals with the right connections.[17]

This segmentation of labor markets is caused by three sets of factors. First, from the supply side, daily wage labor in the urban informal sector usually maintains close links with social networks and informal groups; institutions that provide these people with a cultural and social identity. Moreover, the distinction between wage-employment and self-employment is often so tenuous that labor for hire may also be self-employed in a marginal activity (like peanut selling), where group cohesion is vital. As a result of these features, access even to daily labor for an outsider becomes difficult, if not impossible. One can suggest, therefore, that the lack of contracting alternatives for the urban poor (unlike the rural poor) greatly increases the need for defending one's turf or territory. This reduces the scope of the neoclassical type of labor market where employers can negotiate spot contracts with labor.

Second, from the demand side, employers also face several production risks, briefly discussed in Chapter 2. In labor markets of the urban informal sector, workers are hired for the services of specific skills or behavioral traits they are willing to offer. These services may be highly specialized, say those of a stonecutter or blacksmith, or very general, as of manual labor. As technology is usually nonstandardized and creatively adapted to capital availability, labor does not have a standardized role. At the same time, unlike the rural employer, the urban employer has to be sensitive to fluctuations in market demand for products, which may require variations in the work effort required by labor. Because of these factors, hirers in labor markets may be as interested as those in rural areas in personalizing an employment system, so that terms and conditions of employment can be creatively adjusted.[18]

Third, in urban sector labor markets an employer needs some form of selecting his employees without having access to an institutional mechanism that could screen prospective job seekers. Costs of searching for a worker with a required skill or trait become high. A convenient solution is to contract informally with the social groups to which existing workers belong. The employer not only minimizes search costs, but also gives the screening responsibility to the employees themselves. The arrangement is welcomed on both sides, and often has motivational benefits.[19]

With entry restricted, workers—as in rural markets—are able to sell not only time, but also behavioral and physical endowments. The rents earned for these resources are unpredictable, however, because interlocked markets in a city acquire characteristics similar to those discussed by Bardhan and Rudra while describing labor markets.

A hired worker in a city finds it difficult to use the social group to secure credit in the city. There is some evidence available from developing countries indicating that the social groups try to fulfill some credit needs by forming rotating credit associations of chit funds.[20] In these rotating credit associations, members contribute to a common pool of funds from which each individual takes turns to obtain some credit. These funds are usually inadequate, given the high propensity to consume in cities.

The poor in urban areas, unlike those in the village, do not have many sources of consumption credit. While groups can help in job search and employment, their role as insurance substitutes becomes fairly limited.

Two options are available for a worker in need of credit. If the income earned in a vocation is adequate to take care of his needs (implying no regular earnings gap), he can contract in a manner similar to the rural model by earning tied rents in general bilateral contracts, with employers. If, however, the income earned is inadequate, there are no reliable sources of noninstitutional credit in a city—as there are in a village—to cover the earnings gap. Under these circumstances, workers, may prefer utilizing rents earned from behavioral and physical resources during lean periods as sources of collateral. This idea is somewhat similar to the recent literature on implicit contracts.[21]

The physical (or skill) resource in the urban informal sector also has another implication. Unlike the rural areas, in urban labor markets requirements of physical or skill resource follow a regular, predictable pattern. The physical strength required of a daily laborer carrying heavy loads requires a certain nutritional level. Without the required muscle power, the laborer's productivity will be so low that no employer will be interested in hiring his services.

In conclusion, urban labor markets exhibit a variant of one of the Nurksian vicious circles of poverty. If a person comes to the city with no access to social networks, he has no source of income. If he has no income, the urban food market is prohibitively expensive. This in turn makes him nutritionally deficient, denying him access to even the daily-wage market. Consequently, there is very little scope to find any work.

Housing and Credit Markets

Turning next to the housing and credit markets—as studies have consistently indicated, these service activities show some of the most depressing features of urban poverty. Social networks and informal contracts are not effective in these sectors to secure for members any special privileges. Behavioral relations are dominated by simple bilateral relations because buyers of these services have neither any countervailing power, nor any form of legal protection to prevent exploitation by sellers. In addition, the need to secure such services quickly leads to highly asymmetrical contracts in slum housing and credit markets.

To give an example from the housing market, a slum landlord may offer a small shelter at an exorbitant rate. In Bombay, for instance, a "room"—consisting of loosely fitted corrugated iron sheets— may cost about $3,000. Additional payments have to be made to slum landlords for the use of a water tap, toilets, and electricity. Families live in hovels as small as five feet by five feet under the most appalling conditions. "Filthy toilets, unclaimed garbage and the growing menace of liquor dens" make the physical environment shocking.[22]

From the tenant's perspective, the fact that the city's unorganized markets generate rent-seeking opportunities outweighs the defects in the living environment. As many as 4.5 million people in Bombay and 3 million in Calcutta have to search for shelter in these unhealthy environs. Often, slum landlords use hired toughs to harass these tenants.[23]

In the rural sector the poor had the scope to develop interlinked contracts, but markets for urban credit and slum housing are highly exploitative. So while there are employment opportunities in urban informal sector vocations, the poor have an extremely unsatisfactory quality of life.

Prospects for the Informal Sector

Opinions on the informal sector, quite predictably, have been sharply divided in recent years.[24] One school of thought has emphasized the institutional and technological adaptability displayed by enterprise in unorganized urban markets, and has argued that they can be utilized to diffuse economic growth. This school draws inspiration from the Japanese experience of industrial subcontracting, where small units have created numerous employment opportunities for the work force at minimum transactions costs.[25] The second school, examining mainly the nature of labor markets, takes a more pessimistic view that the urban informal sector is simply a manifestation of poverty.

A compromise view, as expressed by House is perhaps the most appropriate perception of this sector's potential. House does this by subdividing the informal sector into an "intermediate sector" of small manufacturing and business units and a much larger "marginal sector," catering to the service needs of the poor urban consumers.

The conceptual framework developed in this chapter should help in assessing the true potential of the urban informal sector. On a positive side, there is no doubt that by utilizing behavioral relations in both production and exchange, small-scale enterprises have contributed to increases in both private and social wealth. Their institutional flexibility offers a wide range of options for an employment-oriented strategy. Although such enterprises lack the capability of generating large surpluses, they do not have the institutional and organizational inefficiencies associated with large enterprises.[26]

There are, however, some negative features that also have to be considered. Perhaps the most important is that one cannot separate the intermediate sector from the marginal sector. For instance, if a worker is able to find employment in the intermediate sector, he still needs various services such as housing and consumption credit that are not provided by employers in unorganized markets. In marginal vocations, increases in locational rents have also led to a phenomenal growth of hawkers and street vendors causing congestion externalities.[27] The growth of the marginal sector is certainly a manifestation of a country's rural poverty level.

Another negative feature is that although employment and wealth are generated in the urban informal sector, there are no institutional mechanisms available to ensure equitable diffusion. Only workers with access gain, and often, as will be elaborated in Chapter 7, they belong to landed small farmer households—so the benefits become dependent on one's connections and social networks. For those left out of rent-seeking opportunities, total destitution results.

A more practical policy is to encourage *diffuse urbanization*, by which the flexible, adaptive manufacturing enterprises of the informal sector can be encouraged in small rural towns and large villages. This policy involves encouraging industrial subcontracting in rural areas or smaller district or sub-regional towns, so that labor can secure the benefits of economic growth without having to shift residence to overcrowded cities. The growth of the marginal sector in these areas will also be welcome, because this sector will provide supplementary income sources for villagers, without the high civic costs of providing shelter, water supply, and sanitation in cities.

Diffuse urbanization will require investments in improving transport, communications, marketing facilities, and credit in rural areas, as well as suitable fiscal incentives, but this policy would be far less expensive than the massive infrastructural investments required to tackle the manifold problems of urban poverty.

The size of rural populations in developing countries is so large that one cannot expect urbanization to follow the Western experience. It is only by strengthening the growth potential of the rural and rural-industrial sector that these countries can hope to eradicate poverty in the twenty-first century.

Conclusion

The informal organizations in urban areas of less-developed countries present problems as well as some promise. They exhibit considerable segmentation because labor erects entry barriers to prevent others from encroaching on income sources. These barriers are essentially poverty-alleviating institutions that deprive outsiders from a chance of seeking employment opportunities in cities. The greater the poverty in a country, the greater the range of vocations segmented is likely to be.

On the positive side, studies of this sector have consistently indicated the ingenuity and enterprise of informal sector activities. The extent of ingenuity in tapping potential markets has known no bounds, and scarce capital is put to its most productive use. Although one can acknowledge these positive externalities generated by the urban informal sector, there is no escaping the fact that many activities are marginal in nature and reflect a lack of opportunities in villages, rather than access to opportunities in cities.

Appendix A—The Peanut Seller Model

Suppose the seller has the monopoly over territory T. His sales depend on well he can exploit the potential demand over T. Total revenue could be posited to increase at a decreasing rate. This is because as he tries to exploit potential demand further and further away from his stall, his effectiveness in physically attracting attention decreases:

$$\text{Total Revenue:} \quad (pq) = f(t) \qquad (1)$$
$$\text{with } f'(t) > 0, f''(t) < 0$$

Costs of Maintaining Territory

The peanut seller has to defend the territory himself as he has no legal sanction. Assuming that he is too poor to afford a gun or any other material aid, he has to expend a certain level of effort (d) in defending his asset. Effort d could be described as his opportunity cost in terms of energy or effort spent to maintain his clientele.

For every unit of territory the seller defends there are two elements of costs to the seller. First, there is the level of defense effort which he has to undertake physically (d). The further away he goes from the stall the greater is his energy expended just to maintain the defense effort. Second, there is a physical dimension to the problem. The larger the territory, the greater are his opportunity costs in terms of lost sales and lost time when he moves away from the stall, (leaving the stall temporarily unmanned while he is tackling the intruder). So costs per unit of territory could be hypothesized as $t + d$.

$$\text{Defense costs for the seller:} \quad C1(t,d) = t(t + d) \qquad (2)$$

Assume that another person (the intruder) decides to set up a peanut stall. For the intruder, cost of intrusion is dependent on how the existing seller reacts to his presence. If the peanut seller reacts with all the physical violence he can muster, the intrusion may not be worthwhile. If the intruder feels that he can overcome the seller's resistance, he sets up the stall. The model therefore assumes that the seller's reaction and consequent level of violence determine the intruder's decision whether to stake a claim.[28] So for the intruder costs are $C2(t,d) = fl(d)$. It is assumed that the intruder has the same physical strength as the seller. Cost, in the intruder's perception, is the amount of force the seller is going to expend in keeping him away.

Profit Functions and Decision Rule

The profit function is hypothesized to be $(\pi_1, \pi_2 = g(t))$.

The decision rule will be: Peanut seller retains territory if $C1'(t,d) < \pi_1'(t)$. Intruder acquires territory if the reverse inequality holds. This rule states that as long as the marginal profitability is greater than marginal costs, the seller will retain his territory. Once the inequality is reversed, it would not make much sense for him to defend the territory. What this implies is that the seller's intensity of defense would keep declining as one moves toward the outer perimeter of the space T. In other words, the decision to defend or not to defend is made after weighing the net benefits from such action with the effort (physical or otherwise) of taking such a step.

The reasoning behind this decision rule is that the model assumes a leader-follower relation between the peanut seller and the intruder. Owing to intense poverty, opportunity costs of finding regular work are high for both individuals. As long as marginal profitability of exclusion is greater than marginal costs, the incumbent is prepared to use sufficient force to prevent an intrusion. As both individuals are assumed to have the same physical strength, the greater the level of force used by the seller, the less tempting would it be for the intruder to poach on the territory.

Equilibrium Territory

If the level of effort (d) to control his territory is held constant, we can work out the optimal amount of territory or equilibrium territory, t^* for the peanut seller.

As "territory" is simply replacing the quantity variable of conventional economic analysis, derivation of equilibrium conditions is relatively straightforward; t^* can be obtained by setting the marginal revenue from the territory equal to the marginal costs. For analytical convenience we assume that the cost of purchasing peanuts is a constant fraction c of total sales, so equilibrium territory t^* can be worked out as shown in eq. 3.

$$(1 - c)R'(t) - C1'(t,d) = 0 \qquad (3)$$

Two sets of forces are hypothesized to be at work. First, if marginal revenue is large, (likely when demand has high density as in a crowded and busy part of a metropolis like a bus stand or downtown crossing), the vendor will be tempted to increase the control over geographic space. Second, the desire for territorial expansion is checked by increasing marginal costs in defending the territory. The physical effort involved in doing this (d), or the sheer size of t will dampen this desire for increasing the area of controlled turf.

Alternate Technologies
PEANUT SELLERS GRANTED TRADE LICENSE

If the peanut seller gets legal rights, cost curves take a different form. When a vendor is given legal property rights through, say, a licensing system, no one other vendor is allowed to encroach that right by law.

There are, however, costs to be taken into account by the seller. First there is the license fee. This is normally a nominal fixed charge. Second, the seller has to consider the cost of informing the licensing agency of the violation of his legal rights. This cost involves the opportunity costs of foregone business.[29] Assume this cost to be a fixed proportion of total sales, j. Costs of production and complaint to legal authorities now becomes $(c + j)R(t)$.

Legal recognition does not imply that legal enforcement of one's rights is efficient. Whenever a law-enforcing agency is understaffed, as is usual in the case of developing countries, not all complaints of law-abiding citizens can be attended to. One could hypothesize, even in the absence of corruption systems, that authorities will respond only when marginal social benefits of enforcing the law exceed marginal cost of deploying personnel.[30] If, in public officials' perceptions, the marginal social benefit is much less than the marginal social cost, the probability of prompt action (m) would be low. So apart from costs of informing authorities, the seller also has to allow for the fact that legal remedies may not be forthcoming with a probability of $(1 - m)$.

So t^* will depend on the following relations:

$$1 - (c + j) R'(t) - (1 - m)C'(t,d) = 0 \tag{4}$$

with efficient enforcement,

$$m = 1, \text{(iv) gets reduced to } 1 - (c + j) R'(t) \tag{5}$$

Clearly, in this case, the neoclassical solution holds (cost of defending territory does not matter).

If $m = 0$, the solution becomes very similar to eq. 3, except that the term j represents an (unjustifiable) addition to costs. Obviously, this will be an inferior solution to eq. 3.

The term m, representing the probability of legal redress becomes an important factor in making legal recognition appear worthwhile. However, one can think of extreme cases where even when m equals 1, the legal technology (taking a license) may not appear worthwhile. This can happen if the demand for an informal sector activity is extremely inelastic over a territory and j is a large fraction of the sales. As long as there are costs of informing authorities of a legal infringement, there must be a reasonable probability of response by them.[31]

PEANUT SELLERS UTILIZE BEHAVIORAL RELATIONS
TO DEFEND TERRITORY

Two possibilities are likely. First, a behavioral hypothesis could be made that the sellers of the area band themselves together and form a group to protect their common interest and to keep others away. The group could decide that every seller should defend his territory up to the point where marginal revenue equals average costs, with the group providing the balance of effort required. Clearly, with the assumption of rising marginal costs the territory of the seller would be larger under this arrangement. The disadvantage of this solution is that free-rider problems are likely to emerge unless the group has very well-knit social conventions and norms.

A second and more plausible arrangement could be that sellers agree to support one another much more informally in ensuring exclusion. There could be, what has been referred to in property rights literature, as economies of scale in violence.[32] If conventions already exist linking these persons together in general multilateral relations, such arrangements can be costlessly worked out, making outside intrusion more difficult. At the same time, unlike the earlier variant, free-rider problems are less likely to emerge because the group's role in the production technology is relatively easier to define. If a group consists of n individuals, the costs of defending territory become much less because they are shared among all these persons. While the intruder has to reckon with the group's combined level of violence to keep him out, the individual peanut seller shares exclusion costs with the group as a whole, with the effort level divided among the participants.

In these situations two opposing forces are at work. First, all n participants incur costs (opportunity costs of time by leaving their stalls unmanned). In fact, this cost is magnified n times. Second, as a balancing feature, the energy expended in fending off the intrusion is now shared among the n participants and is consequently much lower.

While in theory the first element of cost may appear sizable, in reality the second element reduces costs considerably, because mere threat may be enough to keep out intruders. An intruder would be deterred by the sheer size of the group to which the peanut seller belongs. One could therefore hypothesize that the cost curve for the seller would have a gentler slope than in eq. 2, making the optimal territory the largest. The group therefore is likely to act as an efficient substitute for the legal system.

Notes and References

1. The largest survey using a common methodology has been the study conducted by the International Labour Office. S. V. Sethuraman's *The Urban Informal Sector in Developing Countries* (ILO Geneva, 1981) summarizes the findings of these studies conducted across Asia, Africa, and Latin America. Another view, examining mainly informal labor markets, is by Dipak Mazumdar. See Dipak Mazumdar, "The Urban Informal Sector," in *World Development*, vol. 4, no. 8 (Aug. 1976): 655–679. There has been a plethora of studies by economists, sociologists and anthropologists for many cities in developing countries. This chapter seeks to conceptualize their findings.
2. See Sethuraman, p. 17.
3. See Terence G. McGee, "Peasants in Cities: A Paradox, a Paradox, a most Ingenious Paradox," *Human Organization*, vol. 32, no. 2 (1973): 135–142. Using examples from several countries, McGee argues that members of the informal sector, or "lower circuit," as he calls it, replicate customary norms and behavioral patterns derived from their rural origins.
4. See Owen M. Lynch, "Potters, Plotters, Prodders in a Bombay Slum: Marx and Meaning of Meaning vs. Marx," *Urban Anthropology*, vol. 18, no. 1 (Spring 1979): 1–28.
5. Credit without collateral is obtainable only on very exploitative terms unless specific group-based schemes are implemented by public policy.
6. See William J. House, "Nairobi's Informal Sector: Dynamic Entrepreneurs or Surplus Labor?" *Economic Development and Cultural Change*, vol. 32, no. 2 (Jan. 1984): 277–302, for a description of some of the forms of harassment. The Indian experience is also similar. See Alfred de Souza, ed., *The Indian City* (New Delhi: South Asia Books, 1977).
7. In a developed country even unemployed persons perceive these opportunity costs to be too high in terms of time and effort, so such potential markets are rarely exploited (except perhaps by enterprising school children!).
8. In Calcutta, for instance, sidewalks are neatly apportioned according to the potential demands for products. In a half-mile stretch from Shakespeare Sarani to Victoria Memorial the author encountered the following configuration of hawkers, who occupied the same spots every day for five consecutive weeks: (a) Near the Airconditioned Market (an expensive shopping center)—a magazine stall and a betel nut vendor (selling expensive pans or betel nuts) to the affluent shoppers. (b) One hundred yards west—a vendor selling some inexpensive snacks for a poorer clientele. (c) Near the Birla Planetarium (a tourist spot two hundred yards east)—two push cart vendors, one selling expensive fruit juices (freshly squeezed orange and pineapple juice) and another vending fresh lime (a relatively inexpensive drink). Both had anticipated their poten-

tial demand to be the regular inflow of tourists to the Planetarium. (d) Another few hundred yards east at the Victoria Memorial—at least a dozen vendors each of ice cream, bottled drinks, and different inexpensive snacks and peanuts. (This area is a favorite spot for inexpensive family outings). The vendors confirmed that they had the means of preventing any outsider or rival from intruding into their territory. Very often, pay-offs to the local beat constable doubly ensured their proprietary rights.

9. Of course, the professional tough may sometimes use physical power to transform the arrangement into a patron-client relation. Some of the smuggler "chiefs" of Bombay have such a dubious distinction.

10. See Biswajit Banerjee, "Social Networks in the Migration Process: Empirical Evidence on Chain Migration in India," *Journal of Developing Areas,* vol. 17 (Jan. 1983): 185–196, for an analysis of these processes in the urban informal sector in Delhi. The segmented nature of labor markets is fairly well documented in many other studies. See Mazumdar, "Urban Informal Sector" (note 1).

11. Gay E. Kang and Tai S. Kang, "The Korean Urban Shoeshine Gang: A Minority Community," *Urban Anthropology,* vol. 7, no. 2 (Summer 1978): 171–184.

12. See Asok Mitra, "Calcutta's Backyard–1; Health and Welfare from Garbage," *The Statesman* (Calcutta), January 24, 1984.

13. Anne Bamisaiye, "Begging in Ibadan, Southern Nigeria," *Human Organization,* vol. 33, no. 2 (Summer 1974): 197–202.

14. See Steve Frazier, "A Slum Black Market in Mexico City Is a Part of the Establishment," *Wall Street Journal,* March 25, 1985.

15. See Mazumdar (note 1).

16. Scheduled castes are those castes that have been afforded special rights under the Indian constitution in order to overcome social and economic handicaps they have faced in Hindu society.

17. See John Hariss, "Small Scale Production and Labor Markets," *Economic and Political Weekly,* vol. XVII, nos. 23 and 24 (1982). Papanek and Kontjorojakti have also analyzed similar issues for Jakarta. See Gustav F. Papanek and D. Kontjorojakti, "The Poor of Jakarta," *Economic Development and Cultural Change,* vol. 24, no. 1 (Oct. 1975). Also see Vijay Joshi and Heather Joshi, *Surplus Labour and the City: A Study of Bombay* (New York: Oxford University Press, 1976).

18. An employer has to consider the risks in hiring from an impersonal hiring hall in order to avoid getting a "lemon." See Ackerlof, "Market for 'Lemons.'"

19. This is an important reason for the efficiency observed in informal sector enterprises. See Sethuraman (note 1). The success of the Japanese model of industrial subcontracting could also have been caused by this feature. It also increases the countervailing power of labor.

20. See Donald V. Kurtz, "Rotating Credit Association: An Adaptation to Poverty," *Human Organization,* vol. 32 (Spring 1973): 49–57.

21. See Sherwin Rosen, "Implicit Contracts: A Survey," *Journal of Economic Literature,* vol. 23, no. 3 (1985): 1144–1175.

22. See "Battle of the Budge," *India Today,* September 15, 1985.

23. For a fascinating study of similar issues in the United States, see Peter Stuvyesant, *The Ghetto Marketplace* (New York: Free Press, 1969).
24. See Robert Hackenberg, "New Patterns of Urbanization in South East Asia," *Population and Development Review,* vol. 6, no. 3 (1980), for a summary of these controversies. Also see House (note 6).
25. S. Watanabe, "Entrepreneurship in Small Enterprises in Japanese Manufacturing," *International Labour Review,* vol. 104 (1971): 51–76.
26. See Liebenstein, "X Efficiency" and "On the Economics of Conventions." In X-efficiency, conventions increase deadweight losses within formal organizations. In contrast, conventions are put to productive use in the informal sector.
27. See Biplab Dasgupta, "Calcutta's Informal Sector," *Bulletin,* vol. 5 (1973), Institute of Development Studies, Sussex, for an account of the congestion externalities caused by Calcutta's hawkers.
28. Under conditions of intense poverty and high opportunity costs of finding alternative employment, one can reasonably speculate that turfs and territories will be zealously guarded. An intruder has to expend a great deal of extra strength in order to capture an already occupied rent-seeking opportunity.
29. See Chapter 2 for related discussion. Inefficient enforcement of legal rights often reduces the importance of such rights. The law usually requires the complainant or his attorney to be present.
30. See Chapter 8 for an analysis of corruption systems.
31. This explains the proliferation of petty corruption in most LDCs. If by paying a bribe the individual is able to improve the probability of response m, it might make sound economic sense to include the payoff as a part of costs j. Informal sector participants have to systematically pay off lower-level functionaries of the administration.
32. See Umbeck, *A Theory of Property Rights,* where this idea has been developed in detail.

6

Informal Contracts and Market Structures

The analysis has so far been restricted to unorganized markets of developing countries, but a substantial segment of economic activities also takes place in the organized sector—the two constantly interfacing with one another. For a complete picture, one has to examine the nature of informal contracting processes in the organized markets as well. This chapter proposes a general framework to explain different variations in governance structures in an economy.

The chapter begins by briefly examining how simple bilateral and simple multilateral contracts can also lead to the development of informal property rights or social assets. The next section analyzes some implications of social assets for understanding market forms. The third section develops an analytical framework of market governance structures.

Simple Bilateral and Simple Multilateral Contracts

Economic theory assumes that buyers and sellers transact in markets on the basis of simple bilateral relations, with transactors limiting contracts with each other for specific exchange of goods or services. Modern contract law also recognizes the simplex nature of business contracts.[1] This form of behavioral relations, as discussed earlier, is prevalent in organized sector markets, where public and private sector firms operate in environments similar to those found in developed countries.

Simple bilateral and multilateral relations can generate intangible property rights whenever costs of obtaining information or some unique traits of a seller lead to implicit contracting arrangements.

Simple Multilateral Contracts

Simple multilateral contracts are established when sellers maintain informal relations with a large number of buyers in the market. In these situations, each buyer treats market relations with sellers in terms of single transactions or spot contracts, but continues to return to the same seller in successive time periods, because of the extrapolation principle discussed in Chapter 3. Alternatively, a seller maintains fairly regular relations with a large number of buyers, although each individual buyer transacts business irregularly (as in durable consumer goods). In both examples the seller is able to maintain reasonable expectations of a buyer's patronage, thereby allowing behavioral relations to have a measure of permanence. These relations are fairly similar to the informal contracts discussed in preceding chapters. Accountants have recognized this clientelization as goodwill, and usually impute a value to the sum total of one's clientele when ownership of a business enterprise is transferred.

The word "goodwill" basically describes how a seller is able to acquire access to rent-seeking opportunities with buyers of goods and services. In some cases, personal goodwill arises when an individual is able to maintain simple multilateral relations with large sections of the population.[2] If, for instance, an individual has some unique talent in music or a professional sport, the admiring fans follow predictable behavioral relations, allowing the former to acquire social assets. In other cases, business goodwill is generated when firms in the organized sector are not only able to build a clientele, but transfer these behavioral relations from one time period to another.[3] Simple multilateral relations in the organized sector, often maintained through advertising, could therefore lead to intangible property rights formation.[4]

Even simple multilateral relations could lead to steady streams over successive time periods. Unlike the general variants discussed in earlier chapters, these implicit contracts are created and maintained by investing tangible resources in advertising, product innovation, or lobbying for legal restrictions. Legal norms such as product liability laws also perpetuate these forms of property rights.[5]

These contractual relations imply that if a market appears to have potential for goodwill creation, a firm in the organized sector is likely to invest tangible resources for its development. In the process, any rival informal property rights in the unorganized sector may be quickly destroyed. Some occupations in a village such as pottery making, handloom weaving, and folk entertainment have been severely affected by this feature. In the urban informal sector, locational rents obtained by the poor could also be affected if, for instance, supermarkets are encouraged by public policy makers to replace individually owned shops.

To sum up, simple multilateral relations generate informal property rights in the organized sector of the economy by restricting access to them. As these rights are quickly converted to tangible property, they are virtually indistinguishable from tangible property rights. They may, however, occasionally disturb existing social assets of the poor. A policy maker should be aware of these implications and ensure that suitable compensation is provided for those affected.

Simple Bilateral Contracts

Simple bilateral relations should not normally be expected to generate social assets. However, in labor markets these relations do often create informal property rights because of high costs of information.[6]

Using the terminology of Doeringer and Piore, labor markets in the organized sector can be categorized into *primary* and *secondary* markets. The primary markets have competitive entry points at the time of initial recruitment, and subsequent movement up the job ladder is segmented through internal labor markets. Secondary labor markets are characterized by dead-end jobs, where motivation levels are poor. However, in this sector, turnover—in contrast to the experience in developed countries—is not high because of (a) the relative scarcity of such jobs, and (b) the permanent nature of employment secured in them.[7]

Taking primary markets first, hirers of labor services need a screening mechanism by which labor's quality can be reasonably assessed. There are significant economic benefits in hiring the right person for a job. At the same time, the danger of adverse selection remains, because information available on prospective job seekers is costly to obtain. A convenient solution is to screen on the basis of a person's educational credentials, so the qualitative uncertainty of competence of individual job seekers is circumvented by stressing educational backgrounds and examination scores. Educational institutions with historically good records automatically attract attention of both hirers and prospective job seekers.[8]

Educational institutions consequently are able to create social assets analogous to those of the village laborer. One can speculate that their social assets will be fairly stable over time, so long as they ensure the requisite quality of instruction for their students. Credential-generating capabilities can be affected only if serious structural changes take place either in the economy or in the institution's management.

Students from credential-generating institutions acquire a form of derived social usufructuary rights. These rights are not strictly social assets; they are more in the nature of informal advantages or privileges in Doeringer's terminology. The primary labor market employers themselves often try to convert these privileges into social assets for employees. The growth of internal labor markets, inservice training, and job ladders for these people represents conscious attempts to institutionalize privileges and thereby prevent rapid turnover of skilled personnel within the firm. Apart from employers, employees also use informal social networks, "old boys' networks," and trade unions to perpetuate the rents earned from privileges.

In secondary labor markets, the employer's hiring process has differences when compared with informal labor markets discussed in Chapter 5, because jobs are routine and well standardized. The replacement of an existing worker by another person does not involve major dislocations or costs for the employer. However, as opportunity costs of finding another job are extremely high, workers in these vocations will guard their privileges closely and ensure maximum security of tenure through trade union activities. Entry into dead-end jobs in the organized sector consequently becomes as difficult as entry into informal markets, since the hiring criterion is rarely definable.[9]

The closed nature of the urban employment systems makes the concept of a labor market difficult to define in a developing country. In fact, the analysis suggests that the only market where a job seeker has access to employment through objective criteria is the urban primary labor market. This has consequently put tremendous pressure on educational institutions as more and more persons have sought out educational credentials for jobs in primary labor markets.

Public authorities have been forced to respond to credential seeking by expanding the number of universities and educational institutions. These new institutions have been able to acquire credential-generating capabilities under very limited conditions. These are: (a) when through rapid economic growth hiring requirements in primary markets have shown sufficient incremental demand, and (b) if the institutions have been able to sustain a high quality of instruction. In some cases where (b) has occurred without (a), a brain drain of graduating students to industrialized countries has taken place.

Implications for Market Structures

Rent-generating opportunities exist even in the organized sector. This obviously has theoretical implications in understanding markets, and how economic activities in a country are governed. An understanding of market structures can be facilitated by distinguishing their two dimensions. First, markets represent places of contact between buyers and sellers, a concept well discussed in economic literature. Second, and of equal importance, they also represent methods of contact between these transactors.[10]

Economic models of market structures have followed the neoclassical traditions by focusing attention on the former aspect. Thus, assuming simple bilateral relations, and specifying the conditions under which transactors exchange goods and services, different models of market structures are derived. In these studies, using the idea of separability of the production method from the market for final goods, markets have been taken to be points of contact between buyers and sellers.

If we deny this separability, the concept of the market is altered. As implied all along in this study, buyers and sellers may be as interested in specific forms or methods of contact with each other as they are in the production method because of the rent-generating potentials. In this dimension markets become defined by the prevailing methods of contact.

The methods of contact are influenced by existing informal contracting arrangements. These social relations restrict contact among selected individuals, instead of allowing universal access as assumed in economic theory. A social space becomes definable where the interface between individuals and groups is restricted to persons having well-defined behavioral relations with each other. This feature can be contrasted against the traditional view in economic analysis, where spatial issues have been analyzed in a geographical sense.[11]

Social space becomes a universal feature in all market structures, with the exception of perfect competition. In monopoly, for instance, the social space is controlled exogenously because there is only one seller. In monopolistic competition, resources have to be spent to create and preserve the social space. Rent seeking becomes just a variant where artificial restrictions by public policy reduce the need for other forms of expenditure, and sellers are able to retain control over social space in successive time periods through public regulation.

If informal behavioral contracts are able to successfully limit economic exchange within the social space, two features of interest emerge. First, an average income stream becomes definable, and second, the dispersion of income around this average can also be estimated. One can therefore conclude that the greater the control over social space, the closer will be the resemblance of intangible behavioral relations or social assets to conventional financial assets.

Implications for Governance Structures

The ideas developed so far suggest several implications for the ways in which institutions are organized during economic activity, or to use Williamson's phrase, the governance structure. The *governance structure,* to quote Williamson is "the institutional matrix within which transactions are negotiated and executed."[12]

This definition of governance structures is relevant for transactions taking place within exogenously determined laws, rules, and regulations.[13] The ideas have been developed around the following contracting alternatives.

1. When buyers and sellers trade with markets rather than with each other, the markets of neoclassical economics result. Costless spot contracts allow the Paretian optimality conditions to be fulfilled, and *market governance* results.
2. When, however, long-term complex contracts need to be maintained, transactions costs arise. These costs become significant because there are difficulties in formulating, negotiating, and executing contracts. Each party in the contract tries to behave opportunistically, and negotiates to maximize its payoffs from the long-term relations. In these situations, third-party arbitration can effectively reduce transactions costs. Williamson describes this form as *trilateral governance.*
3. When, in addition, the frequency of exchange between transactors is much higher than in (2), and investments are made that are specific to transactions, *unified governance* emerges. In these situations a hierarchical organization like the modern firm is most appropriate.

In all three forms the governance structure is hypothesized to economize on transactions costs. In the same vein, Pollak has elaborated the conditions under which family governance structures can emerge.

All these forms assume that the finer details of institutional arrangements emerge as economizing responses to transactions costs during market exchange, but in unorganized markets, transactions costs themselves are virtually absent because of the nature of informal contracting processes that are taking place. These implicit contracts effectively monitor exchange relations through social and economic conventions without transactions costs (see Chapter 3). At the same time, however, these contracts have a measure of permanence about them. In a sense, such contracts outline the contours of informal institutions that need to be incorporated into the scheme of governance structures.

A generalized model of governance structures is presented below; it is somewhat different from Williamson's model. Instead of emphasizing transactions costs economies, this model suggests that different governance structures emerge out of market exchange between transactors possessing three forms of property rights. These are (a) tangible property rights, (b) intangible property rights, and (c) labor power, an expression used to describe the purely personal rights each individual has over his or her natural endowments. To begin with, the assumptions of the model are discussed.

The Assumptions

To begin with, assumptions are made to focus attention on critical elements in the model. These assumptions are:

1. Markets are assumed to have a group of buyers and another group of sellers. The term *buyer* defines a person who uses income-generating assets to purchase goods and services. These assets can be money (the most liquid of all assets and the conventional medium of exchange), legal assets, or social assets. The convenience of money is well known as the asset that has no transactions costs attached to it. Legal assets, in contrast, can be used in both their tangible and intangible forms to finance purchases, with varying levels of transactions costs. In addition to these two forms, social assets can also be used to back a person's purchasability.

2. *Sellers* use the rights arising from their assets to design and support their means of production. These assets can be of three forms. First, they may be legal assets, where the legal system clearly defines and protects the existing bundle of rights. The second category covers the rights arising out of social assets or social usufructuary rights. In most of the organized sector and the unorganized sector, individuals and groups acquire such

rights through informal contracts. Finally, a person can utilize the inalienable right over himself or herself in market exchange. This right is termed as arising out of labor power. Labor power refers to supply of labor without any attempt to control the social space. For analytical convenience, a person endowed with labor power is assumed to have no tangible asset except the right over his own person.

3. Buyers and sellers trade in a good or service. The good can be either a product or a factor. It is important to note here that while the different types of assets influence methods of contact between buyers and sellers, the actual transactions of purchase and sale of a good or service are identical to standard economic models. For instance, in the peanut seller example discussed in Chapter 5, the actual market transaction of sale of peanuts is not the issue; the significant feature is that buyers maintain contact with the same sellers.

4. The threefold classification of assets has been made to take into account varying degrees of recognition accorded to them by the legal systems. Legal assets, covering all tangible and intangible assets, are recognized by the legal system. By legal recognition society provides a method of defense of the rights arising from these assets through the judicial system. In contrast, social assets are usually self-policed. Labor power may have legal protection in theory, but rarely in practice because of inefficient enforcement mechanisms discussed in Chapter 2.

5. The assumption that buyers and sellers have one of these forms of assets is obviously a simplifying one. For instance, a landowner can have legal assets such as land, jewelry, and cash in addition to social assets in the village. He may also be the village priest, with his duties in the latter capacity generating steady income.

The Model

The cells in the matrix (Figure 2) describe the resulting forms of market institutions. A brief discussion of each cell follows.

A represents the neoclassical paradigm. When buyers have money and sellers have well-defined ownership rights, Pareto optimality is possible provided transactions costs are zero. When transactions costs are not zero, different forms of governance structures discussed by Williamson are possible. Williamson's model of governance structures analyzes institutions that are created only in this cell.

B is an interesting situation, where only the seller has legal assets.

Sellers

		Legal assets	Social assets	Labor power
Buyers	Money	Neoclassical markets (A)	Restriction-seeking activities (D)	Labor markets (F)
	Social assets	Contracting for future property rights (B)	Reciprocity (E)	
	Legal assets	Barter (C)		

Figure 2. A Matrix of Governance Structures.

Although the buyer has no legal assets, he is able to utilize the informal organization of a group to transact with sellers. As was discussed in Chapter 4, social relations function as a proxy for tangible property rights in providing collaterals. Market exchange can take place in return for a future property right of the buyer, or for a noneconomic good like status. Rural petty business is normally conducted this way in less-developed countries. The village shopkeeper supplies consumer goods required by all villagers in exchange for a promise to pay money back at a later date. Even a landless laborer with no asset, except for the fact that he belongs to the village, is able to purchase consumption goods from the local shop. These relations usually involve the buyer's forgoing claims on future property rights (Chapter 4 has related discussion).

In fact, this feature has been put to use by commercial banks and credit institutions to extend credit to the weaker sections of society in India. To overcome the lack of tangible assets that are needed as collateral for disbursing loans, banks have tried group loan schemes. Under these schemes the poor are allowed credit facilities based on mutual collateral, where a group of landless villagers or street vendors guarantee the bank on each other's behalf.[14] Clearly, the governance structure is quite different from the neoclassical model.

In *C,* when both buyers and sellers have legal assets, transactions can take place only through barter. Of course, when legal assets are relatively liquid, transactions in this cell will begin to resemble *A.*

Cell *D* is hypothesized to be the most common governance form in developing countries. Buyers have legal assets while sellers have social assets. Sellers are able to exercise their social usufructuary rights to exclude other potential entrants into the market. Although, the focus has been primarily on developing countries, this form could in fact be equally applicable to industrialized countries.

Transactions in this form are quite different from A because markets exhibit different degrees of segmentation. The endogenously created restrictions generate economic rents to beneficiaries.[15]

When restriction seeking becomes the predominant feature of the economy, conventional microeconomic theory may no longer be the appropriate means of analysis. For instance, in the neoclassical framework factors are paid the value of their marginal products. Economists have argued for long that the marginal product rule is inappropriate for developing countries with excess labor supply as it implies wage rates to close to zero. From this analysis, it can be seen that earnings depend on the nature of rent-sharing arrangements through implicit contracts rather than on the basis of simple bilateral relations implied by the marginal productivity theory.

The concept of reciprocity in E has usually been used by economic anthropologists to explain economic relations between individuals in primitive societies that are based on status rather than on contract.[16] Reciprocity is an important form of governance for families, and sometimes even for larger social groups.

Intrafamily transactions invariably involve all transactors' having social assets. A father may give his daughter an expensive gift and in exchange receive her love. The prodigal son may be welcomed back home with the family insuring him from destitution. The sharing of domestic work betwen spouses could be yet another example of reciprocity.

Reciprocity is also observable among larger social groups. In many African societies, for instance, as Sarah Berry has observed, property rights appear to be politicized rather than privatized.[17] Leaders of business and politics invest resources in mobilizing sectional rights and loyalties. A wage earner in organized sector employment in a city retains his rights in the village, and in turn has to reciprocate the hospitality when kinsmen visit the city. These are also forms of reciprocity, except that the group is larger than the family. Even in Asian and Latin American societies, larger groups maintain reciprocal social relations. These relations provide insurance against individual risks.[18] If there is a localized crop failure for a farmer, reciprocity ensures financial assistance from the larger community. Of course, compared to the family—where altruism plays a major role—

reciprocity in larger groups in unorganized markets will be relatively less.

Families also often use their collective strength to produce goods and services. In such cases they use their social assets in production, and have a governance structure indistinguishable from D. In fact, as free-rider problems are fewer compared with a larger social group, their capacity to exploit rent-seeking opportunities will be much more.

F represents labor markets of conventional economics. If labor is scarce relative to demand, neoclassical marginal productivity theory may apply. If labor is in abundance relative to demand, wages would be reduced to a subsistence level, as most economic theories predict.

Conclusion

An understanding of the nature and forms of social assets enhances the knowledge of economic institutions in developing countries. This chapter has suggested that informal institutions that arise out of regular behavioral relations govern transactions in unorganized markets. In the next three chapters, some economic and policy implications of these institutions are discussed.

Notes and References

1. Ian R. Macneill, "The Many Futures of Contracts," *Southern California Law Review*, vol. 47, no. 3 (May 1974): 691–816, distinguishes among neoclassical contracts, classical contracts, and relational contracts. Relational contracts are closest to simple bilateral and multilateral contracts.
2. An excellent summary of the development of goodwill from an accounting perspective is available in Hugh P. Hughes, *Goodwill in Accounting: A History of the Issues and Problems* (Athens: Georgia State University, 1982).
3. Accountants measure purchased goodwill against our interest in internally developed or nonpurchased goodwill. Accounting literature ignores the latter form of goodwill. See *Accounting for Goodwill* (Accountants International Study Group, 1975).
4. One can think of advertising and other promotional measures erecting barriers to entry for potential entrants (thus creating social assets) while simultaneously protecting existing social assets from depreciating. See William S. Comanor and Thomas A. Wilson, *Advertising and Market Power* (Cambridge: Harvard University Press, 1974).
5. See Ronald McKean, "Products Liability: Implications of Some Changing Property Rights," in Furubotn and Pejovich, *The Economics of Property Rights*. A system of caveat venditor (seller beware), in fact, allows sellers

to generate informal property rights through risk-pooling. McKean in contrast discusses the property rights implications for buyers.

6. Screening processes are necessary to avoid adverse selection problems. See Ackerlof "Market for 'Lemons.'"

7. See Peter B. Doeringer and Michael J. Piore, *Internal Labor Markets and Manpower Analysis* (Lexington: D.C. Heath, 1971). In the Doeringer-Piore model developed for the United States, turnover in the dead-end jobs is very high. In developing countries the jobs of office peons, office security guards, messengers, chauffeurs, etc, are highly sought after, as they have security of tenure through legislation and growth of trade unionsm.

8. See Mark Blaug, "Human Capital Investment: A Slightly Jaundiced Survey," *Journal of Economic Literature*, vol. 14, no. 2 (Sept. 1976), for a summary of related literature in human capital theory.

9. Jobs in this section are highly standardized and require very little if any skill. The hiring process is complicated by precisely this feature. As Mazumdar ("The Urban Informal Sector") has shown, entry into this sector becomes extremely difficult. Institutions like employment exchanges are unable to function efficiently, as they are able to provide jobs for only a fraction of the waiting lists in their live registers. The backlog of names is so large that these registers have ceased to have much relevance in job search.

10. See Peter O. Steiner, "Markets," *International Encyclopaedia of Social Sciences*, vol. 9 (1968): 575–581.

11. See Robert D. Dean, William H. Leahy, and David L. McKee, *Spatial Economic Theory* (New York: Free Press, 1970).

12. Oliver E. Williamson, "Transactions Costs Economics, the Governance of Contractual Relations," *Journal of Law and Economics*, vol. 22, no. 2 (Oct. 1979): 233–262.

13. Robert Pollak ("A Transactions Cost Approach") has sought to analyze families as a governance structure. The model developed in this chapter, however, offers a different viewpoint, by suggesting that a family can be *used* to promote restriction-seeking activities.

14. Group-based savings and credit programs are now being encouraged even by commercial banks. The analysis of contracting for future property rights is discussed in Chapter 4.

15. Most literature on rent seeking has developed around the idea that in dividuals in an economic system waste resources competing for rents from exogenously determined restrictions (such as quotas). This study proposes instead that rents arise from endogenous informal contracts, and are in the nature of restriction seeking. See James Buchanan et al., *Towards a Theory of Rent Seeking Society*.

16. See George Dalton, *Research in Economic Anthropology*, vol. 4 (New York: Jai Press), particularly pages 1–12.

17. Sara S. Berry, "The Food Crisis and Agricultural Change in Africa, A Review Essay," *African Studies Review*, vol. 27, no. 2 (1984): 59–112.

18. An interesting account of reciprocity in a tribal community in India is discussed by K. L. Kothari, *Tribal Social Change in India* (Udaipur: Himanshu Publications, 1985).

7

Social Assets
and Rural-Urban Migration

The previous chapters have developed the theme of how social assets outline the contours of informal institutions. This chapter proceeds to examine implications for rural-urban migration. Migration from villages to cities is suggested to take place following microeconomic decisions by individuals to either alter or add to their portfolio of informal and formal property rights.

The chapter is divided into four sections. To begin with, an exploratory analysis is conducted to demonstrate the links between poverty and migration. This is followed in the second section by an analysis of the forms of migration. In the third section, a simple microeconomic model of migration is formulated using the tools of portfolio theory. This section describes a model that takes into account some institutional perspectives in migratory processes. The final section simulates some results using the model.

Migration is viewed as involving the physical movement of individuals with different portfolios of legal and social assets in search of superior earning opportunities. The ultimate decision to migrate or not migrate is postulated to be a microeconomic one made by each person after weighing the costs and benefits of changing a portfolio of assets.

Urbanization and the Influx of the Poor

The Received Theory

Migratory patterns have followed similar paths in most parts of the developing world. Individuals belonging to landless families and marginal farm households come to cities retaining some social groupings such as tribes, kinship ties to secure access to income streams in the urban informal sector. At the same time, people from more affluent rural families also move to cities to invest in educational credentials with expectations of changing their social space.

Economic analysis of migration has been gradually responding to the unfolding complexities of migratory processes revealed by empirical work over the last three decades. It is useful to outline briefly the changing perceptions of migration of economists since the 1950s.

In the late fifties and early sixties the Lewis-Ranis-Fei type of models were quite mechanistic in their analysis of labor in developing countries, and did not recognize the complexities of rural-urban migration. Their emphasis was instead on suggesting how rural surplus labor could be utilized as an industrial work force. Implicit in this argument was the assumption that this labor would have to shift residence to industrial centers.[1]

By the late sixties, however, it became apparent that rural labor was coming to cities in large numbers. An explanation given for this influx was that these people came to cities in search of a better future. Migration was therefore explained as an inevitable implication of prevailing levels of poverty and overpopulation. A key element in a migration decision function was postulated to be a rural-urban wage differential.

The Harris-Todaro model sought to formalize these features. In addition, this model gave explicit recognition to two urban institutional features. These were (a) institutionalized urban formal or organized sector wages and (b) the presence of a large urban informal sector, which performed the role of a waiting hall for the migrants who had expectations of securing formal sector employment.[2]

The Harris-Todaro model has again been followed by several studies of both the migratory process and the urban informal sector in developing countries. These have revealed two sets of issues.[3] First, in the overpopulated countries of South Asia, migration flows have been consistently smaller than the Harris-Todaro model predicted. Second, or perhaps a cause of the these relatively small flows, has been the segmented nature of the receiving sector, the urban informal sector.

The migration literature continues to modify and alter models based on the paradigm that urban prospects are tied to wage-employment possibilities in urban labor markets.[4] This feature is apparent in modifications to the Harris-Todaro model, made notably by Harris and Sabot, Stark, and Knight and Bannerjee, where the roles of job

search, information, and remittances in the migratory process have
been recognized while retaining the wage-employment paradigm. The
earlier chapters have, however, argued that in unorganized markets
behavioral relations generate informal property rights, which restrict
entry access to most labor markets. Thus while a labor market exists
in theory, in practice every person actually has differentials in access
to segmented labor markets.

If these institutional features of unorganized markets are recognized, some conventional wisdom of the migration literature can be
questioned. To mention a few: (a) Employment possibilities in the
organized sector becomes a remote likelihood for a poor migrant;
(b) job search within the urban informal sector for a newcomer is
expensive because information is rarely allowed to filter out of groups
who control entry access; and (c) job search for a member of a group
with general multilateral relations does not involve high costs. These
new features can be incorporated by postulating that migration decisions from rural to urban areas are taken after weighing the risks
and returns of different types of tangible and intangible property
rights.

Rural-Urban Migration and Informal Institutions

This chapter can be viewed as giving another perspective on migration. The points of departure from some recent conventional models
are basically twofold. First, the entire economy as an employment
system is viewed as consisting of a number of segmented markets,
where informal contracting processes limit access to jobs in unorganized markets and secondary labor markets of the unorganized
sector. In primary labor markets of the organized sector, employment can be secured only upon fulfilling a definite criterion.[5] A migrant without suitable access has thus very little chance of securing
employment in the urban informal sector. Second, social assets as an
institutional feature are explicitly recognized. As the segmentation
has already been discussed at length, an elaboration of the implication of social assets is undertaken below.

Poverty, as discussed earlier, while implying a lack of tangible
property rights, is usually alleviated through complex contracting
processes that generate social assets for the concerned person. When
a person moves to the city, his migration decision cannot be based
on simply assessing the possibilities of securing urban employment
and wages; he has, in fact, to weigh the opportunity costs of forgoing
existing interlinked living arrangements worked out in the village for

the actual social assets available in the city. In this sense, migration even of the poor involves altering a given portfolio of property rights.

For affluent people, the considerations are likely to be qualitatively different. Here, migration is caused by an expectation of changing one's social space. The expectation is to acquire social assets through job property rights in the organized sector, which can supplement an existing portfolio of rural tangible property rights. In fact, the present formulations of migration models, relying as they do on probabilistic beliefs, are more appropriate in explaining migration decisions of such affluent, propertied individuals.

So rural-urban migraiton is hypothesized to be caused by the desire of individuals to increase their possession of income-generating assets. These assets can be legal assets, social assets, or a portfolio of legal and social assets.

As social assets create social usufructuary rights that cannot be transferred, individuals having just social assets in villages will incur higher opportunity costs than persons having legal assets (such as land).[6] One can predict that individuals owning some legal assets (such as small and medium landowners) will move more readily to cities to develop social assets as supplements to their inadequate legal assets.

An Analysis of Forms of Migration

Migration and Social Space

Theories of migration have defined migration as movement across regions in search of gainful employment. As we have seen earlier the concept of space itself has both a geographic and social dimension, while migration results in a physical movement across geographic space, it may or may not involve movement across social space.[7] Migration is postulated to involve one of the following possibilities:

Type X Migration: Searching for a job outside a geographic space but within the same social space. For instance, a Sicilian may arrive in New York's Little Italy in search of employment.

Type Y Migration: Searching for jobs outside a social space, but within a geographic space. A person may look for a job outside the social network or group he or she is normally associated with. Strictly speaking, this form is not really migration. However, with improved transportation the geographic space becomes much larger.

Type Z Migration: Searching for a job outside both geographic and social space. (A Connecticut Yankee in King Arthur's Court could be an example of this.) When a landowner with educational credentials moves to a city, he expects to secure employment outside his usual geographic and social space.[8]

Migration by the poor is of Type X, where opportunity costs are not high because they continue to remain in the same social space. Type Z usually involves the relatively affluent villagers who utilize education to move to cities in the hope of securing permanent job property rights in primary labor markets of the organized sector. Migration models like the Harris-Todaro model therefore have most relevance for Type Z form of migration. Type X, by contrast, has the migrant moving physically without losing the structural strength of his social group. He has easy access to the group's earning capabilities, as well as almost perfect information on job prospects.

Circular migration is of Type Y, and opportunity costs in this form are low because the migrant retains close links with rural institutions, and may, in fact, also be participating in informal contracts in rural labor markets. As communications between a hinterland and a city improve, the rural poor can spend a part of their time in the city supplementing their rural income. These activities typically have very low returns and are itinerant in nature. In suburban Calcutta, for instance, rapid intraregional rail transit has extended the city's immediate hinterland to about 1000 square miles.

Circular migration does not impose a heavy strain on the civic system as in the case of Type X and Type Z migration. In fact, it can be viewed as a welcome development by which the rural poor can share some fruits of urban economic growth.

Voluntary and Involuntary Migration

One other important factor of this approach is to recognize a qualitative aspect of migration. There could be situations when involuntary migration of Type Z takes place because of a collapse of the rural economic system. The whole set of rural economic entitlements may collapse, as Sen has analyzed for the Great Bengal famine of 1949 and the Sahel areas have experienced recently. War, famine, or pestilence may break down rural entitlements, and lead to a massive exodus of the poor from rural areas. This migration is involuntary migration, in contrast to voluntary migration, where the migrant hopes to improve his asset portfolio.[9] The former takes place when all poverty-alleviating institutions collapse in the countryside. The latter, in contrast, is caused by the desire of individuals to improve their portfolio of income-generating assets. When an individual seeks out city life, after being attracted by the wealth of the metropolis, his relative poverty has attracted him to the city.[10] When in contrast, his migration decision is caused by a breakdown of rural entitlements, his absolute poverty has pushed him out of the village.

The essential difference between these two types of migration is a difference in motivating factors. The welfare and policy implications will obviously be very different. A policy maker should view the prevention of involuntary migration as one of the central planks of developmental policy. Voluntary migration, in contrast, is extremely expensive to prevent unless rural employment and income opportunities for the poor are improved.

Before developing these ideas into a migration model, it will be useful to get a perspective on the scale of rural-urban migration. As Michael Lipton has observed, gross rural-urban migration in the 1950s was only 3 percent of the rural population in South Asia, 6 percent in East Asia, and 7 percent in Africa. According to the Indian census of 1961, only 4.2 percent of Indians were rural-born townsmen. Later figures indicate similar trends in most countries.[11] Migration can therefore be inferred to be an exception rather than a rule for the rural poor.

The Model

The Assumptions

To begin with, it will be useful to list the assumptions under which the model holds. These are:

1. Most migrants are poor. They belong to landless and marginal farm households. Even affluent villagers feel themselves to be relatively poor compared to affluent urbanites.
2. The rural poor are on the lookout for acquiring income-generating assets. As poverty precludes them from owning conventional legal assets, they seek social assets or entitlements. These assets have to yield income quickly as these people have no savings to finance a job search.
3. The acquisition of social assets by the poor merely alleviates the problem of insufficient income; it does not make a person affluent.

4. Social assets generate social usufructuary rights. These rights cannot be traded or easily delegated.
5. Jobs in primary labor markets of the organized sector require minimum educational qualifications.[12]
6. In the urban informal sector, job openings are severely restricted by informal groups and informal contracting processes.
7. If a person comes to a city without social connections, to acquire social assets the migrant must be acceptable to an existing entitlement group. Previous contacts with the group can reduce the time he has to wait to be accepted. In a broader sense, the potential migrant's perception of the time required to acquire social assets depends on his subjective calculation of how quickly he can get accepted. Family members and kinsmen will naturally require no waiting time. Misinformation can sometimes make a person without social connections alter his or her perception of the speed of being accepted by the social group.
8. Every person is assumed to work equally hard to generate income from urban entitlements. Occupations based on these social assets generate income from self-employment or wage employment with no legal protection and therefore depend on a person's capacity to work.

Analysis

A MEAN-VARIANCE MODEL OF MIGRATION

The analysis utilizes a mean-variance model to explain the nature of migration (see Appendix B for mathematical derivations). This model has been traditionally used by economists to analyze the portfolio of financial assets individuals are likely to invest in. Two factors influence a person's choice of portfolio. First, an assessment has to be made of the expected returns or the likely returns from an asset. Second, the risk has to be assessed by calculating the variance or dispersion around the expected return. For instance, if an asset has a high expected return and high variance, there are likely to be fluctuations in the average returns for an investor, implying that while returns may be high one year, they may be very low the next year. If, in contrast, both expected returns and variance are low, the asset can be expected to yield low but steady returns.

Using a similar analogy, prospective migrants choose a portfolio of legal and social assets. A move to the city seeks to supplement the meager rural income generating assets with earnings from urban social assets. Unlike the financial investor however, the migrant has to

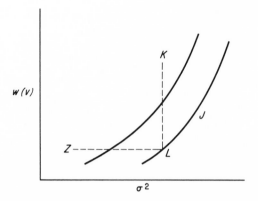

Figure 3. Migration Possibilities.

decide how he is to allocate time between the town and the village and simultaneously maximize his portfolio of income-generating assets. His choices are described in Figures 3 and 4, where $w(v)$ and σ^2 represent the migrant's assessment of expected income and variance respectively.

The indifference curves shown in the figures represent his perceptions of a trade-off between the expected return and the variance. The line ZLK represents the actual trade-off opportunities. For example, if he remains in the village, he is in a low risk environment, where expected returns from social and legal assets are low, combined with low variance in income (shown by Z). By moving to the city, he may be able to increase his expected income, but simultaneously also faces risks of variations in that income. The reverse L shape implies that the migrant has a choice of remaining either in

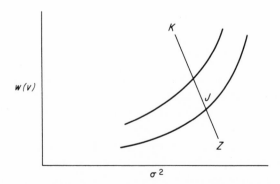

Figure 4. The Harris-Todaro Model Revisited.

the rural area (Z) or in the city (K). If the village is close to the city he may, however, be able to allocate his time between the rural and urban areas.

The migration decision is taken if by moving to the city a person is able to increase the value of his portfolio of assets. This can occur if (a) by moving to the city he is able to supplement the legal and social assets, or (b) income from the urban social assets is considerably higher than foresaken rural social assets (applicable for landless laborers). Analogous to an investor, the migrant then has to weigh the average income he hopes to receive from urban social assets against its likely variance over time.

The Harris-Todaro model can be described in the mean-variance approach as involving a variation in the trade-off line. In the urban organized sector, expected earnings are higher and variance in this income is lower than in a village because of job security. In such cases, a migrant will predictably spend all his time in the city aspiring for urban income from the organized sector.

K being to the left of Z implies that income streams from organized sector jobs have higher means and lower variances because of the regularity of remuneration in these employment systems (see analysis of organized sector labor markets in Chapter 6). Interestingly, even if a migrant has no clear knowledge of the probability of securing a job, he might still migrate as long as $w(v)$ is marginally above indifference curve passing through Z in Figure 4.[13] This form of migration is appropriate for owners of tangible property rights who seek to supplement their legal assets. This solution, however, is not appropriate for the landless poor, for whom leaving the village will result in a loss of their rural social assets. For such persons moving out of the village means losing the income represented by the Z in Figure 4.

Some General Observations

Migration depends on the valuation of urban income and variation in that income as perceived by the migrant. These assessments are made on the basis of information available to the person. If a migrant belongs to the same social space as others controlling an earning opportunity, his access to income will be virtually identical with what is already available with the group. His subjective valuation of job opportunities appears much less probabilistic than assumed in the Harris-Todaro model.

The model does not account for a person who uses the informal sector as a steppingstone for a formal sector job. This type of mobility is restricted because of the segmented nature of markets. However, there have been cases of migrants using their social assets in cities to educate their children, and thereby enable them to acquire social and economic mobility to move to the formal sector. Migrants with sufficient motivation have been known to utilize urban opportunities (like night schools) to acquire suitable credentials for jobs in the organized sector. In some informal sector activities where income is high (notably crime), quick conversion to tangible property is undertaken, and credentials are sought thereafter to move up the social ladder.

Simulations

Variations in Discount Rate

If the landless poor view present actual earnings from rural social assets to be more important than a more speculative expected earnings by moving to the city, their valuation of expected wage gets lower. Consequently for such persons a move to the city is unattractive unless a job is assured on arrival there. However, a landless worker may sever his rural connections because of possibility of urban employment.[14] Such people move to urban areas but find employment opportunities closed out in the urban informal sector.

A Breakdown of Rural Entitlements

This reduces landless agricultural workers' expected rural wage w (v). In terms of Figures 5a and 5b, Z' becomes unattainable, consequently reducing their costs of relocating from the village to the city. The trade-off line shifts to the left, toward the origin in the graph. Migration may or may not occur depending on (a) the individual's degree of risk aversion, and (b) how he evaluates the mean and variance of urban income (represented by K'' in Figures 5a and 5b). Most governments have tried to legalize some social assets (laws against evicting sharecroppers, mandatory relief schemes during lean seasons, etc). These measures act as brakes to involuntary migration, by reducing the value of K'' (Figure 5a).[15]

If the entire system of rural entitlements collapses there would be involuntary migration as indicated in Figure 5b. This would corre-

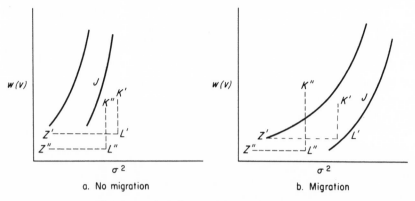

a. No migration   b. Migration

Figure 5. Migration and Rural Entitlements.

spond to Sen's description of the Great Bengal famine, or the Sahel famine in Africa when many persons left their villages for urban areas in search of food.

Introduction of Modern Technology in Agriculture

The green revolution has, as seen in Chapters 3 and 4, increased the countervailing power of labor, and generated new general bilateral contracting possibilities in villages.[16] In terms of Figure 3, Z moves up relative to K. So rural-urban migration will become less attractive. However, if a portion of the middle peasantry experiencing marginalization of land holdings are not able to secure improvements in productivity of their property rights, migration by this group will continue.[17]

An interesting corollary to the green revolution has been the appearance in some of these relatively affluent farming regions of an informal sector of landless laborers from poorer regions. Such people derive social assets from landowners who hire their cheap labor for work on farms and homes that was earlier performed by the local poor.[18] These regions end up having two distinct wage rates—one for local labor and one for migrant labor. Social assets are quickly formed, with the same set of worker being hired every year.

Circular Migration

The concept of circular migration can be analyzed by dropping the assumption that rural social assets have to be forsaken by the mi-

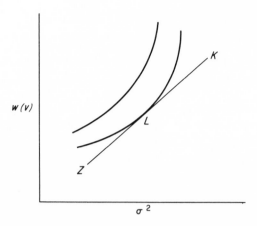

Figure 6. Circular Migration.

grant. The trade-off line takes the form shown in Figure 6. The optimum point is the tangency between the trade-off line and the highest indifference curve indicating that the migrant is best off by spending a part of the time in the city and a part of the time in the village.

If social assets in a village are well protected through customary norms, as in many African societies, rural-urban migration across large distances would be of this type. Each tribal group may send its educated youths to the city in search of jobs so that the *whole* group's portfolio of assiets is increased. In return the migrant's customary economic rights in the distant village get protected.

Conclusion

The chapter has sought to integrate rural-urban migration with some of the ideas discussed previously. Migration of the poor, as in conventional analysis, has been demonstrated to be caused by individuals and groups seeking out a better life in cities. Where the analysis has differed is in the sources of motivation, and in describing the migrant's decision-making process. This analysis has sought to explain migration decisions by understanding the nature of informal institutions that delineate the rights of access to income and work.

Appendix B—The Mean Variance Migration Model

Assume that the prospective migrant is a risk-averse individual who hopes to receive an income stream Y from his assets (legal, social, or both). Using the expected utility theory, his indifference map between expected income and variance of income can be derived.

$$\text{Let } U(Y) = bY + cY^2, b\, 0, c < 0, b + cY > 0 \tag{1}$$

$$\text{Taking expectations, } E[U(Y)] = bEY + cE(Y^2) \tag{2}$$

Keeping $EU(Y)$ at a constant level M, the indifference map between expected income and the variance in income can be derived.

$$M = bEY + cEY^2$$
$$M = bw + cw + c\sigma^2, \text{ where } E(Y) = w, \text{ variance of income } = \sigma^2. \tag{3}$$

These indifference curves give the individual's subjective trade-off between expected income and variance in income.

Next is the formulation of the budget line or the actual trade-off a person faces. Depending on social and institutional factors, the trade-off line can give a range of solutions to cover the whole spectrum of migration.

Income the individual can get from his portfolio of assests can have the following forms:

$$Y = Yr \tag{4}$$

$$Y = Yu \tag{5}$$

$$Y = Yu + Yr \tag{6}$$

Equation 4 is appropriate for a person living in the village and securing income from a legal of a social asset. This category covers income from rural social or legal assets for group A or marginal and small farmers, and income from only social assets for group B or landless laborers, Eq. 5 is relevant for a person who has forsaken his or her rural social asset for an urban social asset (from group B). Equation 6 is relevant for a migrant to the city who supplements his or her rural legal asset with an urban entitlement (group A), after delegating the management of his rural asset to a relative.

The expected income will consist of any of the following forms: $w(r)$—the rural expected income when the person is in the villlage; $w(r)^*$—expected rural income when the person leaves the village. Obviously, $(w(r)^*)A > (w(r)^*)\, B = 0$. $W(u)$ denotes the expected urban income. Total expected income is denoted by w.

$$w = w(r) \qquad \text{Group A or B (non-migrant)} \tag{7}$$

$$w = w(r)^* + w(u) \quad \text{Group A} \tag{8}$$

$$w = w(u) \qquad \text{Group B} \tag{9}$$

The underlying assumption is that the average wage in rural areas and in the urban informal sector is known to every one and is normally distributed. In rural areas, at a given level of development, farmers have a fairly well-developed sense of the expected or average income. This income has a variance of σ_r^2 through natural factors such as weather, floods, drought, etc. When an individual delegates his asset to a relative, although the coefficient of variation remains the same, variance will decrease to σ_r^{2*}.

In an analogous manner, in the urban informal sector, incomes have considerable variations. These may be due to (a) entirely exogenous factors such as the cyclical nature of economic activity, or periodic raids by civic authorities and the police, and (b) natural factors such as the weather and seasonal climate. The variation in urban informal sector income is denoted as σ_u^2.

In the urban organized sector as a regular permanent job is secured, this variation is assumed to be zero. Total variation that is subjectively assessed can take away any of the following forms:

$$\sigma^2 = \sigma_v^2 \qquad \text{Group A or B} \qquad (10)$$
$$\sigma^2 = \sigma_{r*}^2 + \sigma_U^2 \ \text{Group A} \qquad (11)$$
$$\sigma^2 = \sigma_u^2 \qquad \text{Group B} \qquad (12)$$

The next step is to define how the potential migrant evaluates these choices. The crucial element in the model is the migrant's evaluation of expected urban income. His decision to migrate or not to migrate depends on a subjective assessment of the costs and benefits of the move.

It is here that the model departs from conventional portfolio theory. Unlike the normal investor, a migrant moves to supplement his meager rural income from urban social assets. While an investor has to make a portfolio decision on how time should be allocated to improve the portfolio of income-generating assets. Obviously, except in the case of circular migration, the time choice becomes a discrete one—between living in a city and living in the village.

The migrant's decision between the city and the country is also influenced by his perception of relocation costs. There are many real and psychological costs associated with a movement of this nature. They cover, apart from what has already been discussed, transport costs, urban environmental costs (bad housing, poor work conditions, difficulties in obtaining consumption credit), and costs of consumption during job search.

These perceptions affect the migrant's valuation of expected urban income $w(u)$. His valuation of $w(u)$ will depend on two sets of factors. They are:

1. the speed with which $w(u)$ can be reached. The waiting time t to reach $w(u)$ will spell destitution for him. Assuming a discount rate of r, the expected urban wage becomes $w(u)\bar{e}^{rt}$. If the entitlement is assured on arrival in a city for migrants with social connections, $t = O$, $w(u)\bar{e}^{rt} = w(u)$, implying that work is available for the asking. Every day of waiting time (t), will progressively lower his valuation of expected wage, at a given discount rate.

2. Relocation costs c. These include all the opportunity costs discussed earlier of shifting residence to the city.

The final valuation of expected income $w(v)$ is likely to be: $w(v) = w(r)^* + w(u)\bar{e}^{rt} - c$. In Figure 3, Z represents the mean-variance combination for a nonmigrant. When a person weighs the option of migration to a city, his perceived trade-off line is represented by ZLK. K represents his total valuation of mean and variance from both rural and urban incomes. It should be at a point above the indifference curve, passing through J for migration actually to take place.

Notes and References

1. See W. Arthur Lewis, "Economic Development with Unlimited Supply of Labour"; Gustav Ranis; and John Fei, "A Theory of Economic Development."

2. See John R. Harris and Michael P. Todaro, "Migration, Unemployment and Development: A Two-Sector Analysis," *American Economic Review*, vol. 60 (1971): 126–142.

3. Several such studies are available for countries in Africa, Asia, and Latin America using wage data. Studies analyzing the specific institutional role of the urban informal sector in the migration process have not been common. One exhaustive study of this aspect has been conducted for Delhi by Biswajit Banerjee. See Biswajit Banerjee, "The Role of the Informal Sector in the Migration Process: A Test of Probabilistic Migration Model and Labour Market Segmentation for India," *Oxford Economic Papers*, vol. 35 (1983): 399–422. There are no studies for other institutional aspects of migration.

4. See *Migration and the Labor Market in Developing Countries*, Richard H. Sabot, ed. (Boulder, Col.: Westview Press, 1982), for a collection of some leading contributions to this subject, particularly the article by John R. Harris and Richard H. Sabot, "Urban Unemployment in LDCs: Towards a More General Search Model." In the Harris-Sabot model, for instance, as with most migration models, informal institutions are viewed as exogenous to the migration process.

5. Most literature adheres to the assumption that the informal sector retains its properties of being a waiting hall for job searchers. See V. H.

Joshi, "Rural-Urban Migration, Urban Unemployment and Economic Development" (Lecture at the Center for International Studies, Harvard University, April 24, 1981), where the author summarizes related literature. Dipak Mazumdar, in "Segmented Labor Markets in LDCs," *American Economic Review*, vol. 73, no. 2: 254–259, has, however, shown that labor markets in the organized sector are segmented from the informal sector. We have, however, argued that markets even within the informal sector are highly segmented because of the nature of informal contracting processes (see Chapter 5, the peanut seller model, for related analysis).

6. Where customary norms retain their importance, as in some of the tribal communities of Africa and Asia, rural social assets need not be forgone on leaving the village. Social assets in villages acquire strong resemblance to legal assets. This could be one explanation for noticeably higher migration trends and circulatory migration in these countries—every person in the rural community can try his luck in the city.

7. See Leszek A. Kosinsky and Mansell R. Prothero, ed., *People on the Move* (London: Methuen, 1972), particularly articles by R. J. Pryor, G. Krishnan, and G. S. Kosal, and the Introduction.

8. Educational credentials provide access to a higher social space, although they do not guarantee entry. See Chapter 6 for related discussion.

9. See Amartya K. Sen, "Poverty and Famine."

10. The distinction drawn here differs from push and pull migration used in the literature. Joshi (note 5), for instance, describes pull migration as the result of attraction of higher wages in the city, and push migration as being caused by the lack of gainful work in the village. In this book any person coming to develop or utilize social assets in a city is a voluntary migrant. Involuntary migration, by contrast, takes place only if there is a collapse of rural entitlements.

11. See Michael Lipton, "Migration from Rural Areas of Poor Countries: The Impact on Rural Productivity and Income Distribution," in Sabot, ed.

12. Credential seeking has reached such proportions in India that it is not uncommon to find graduates in dead-end jobs.

13. Affluent migrants who normally do this are financed during their urban sojourn by rural legal assets.

14. If an additional assumption is made that the landless are more risk-averse, their indifference curves will become steeper, making migration even more unattractive.

15. In an article critiquing the Harris-Todaro model, Bhagwati and Srinivasan have argued for taking steps to increase rural wages. Our argument here calls for the strengthening of rural entitlement systems. See Jagdish N. Bhagwati and T. N. Srinivasan, "On Reanalyzing the Harris-Todaro Model: Policy Rankings in the Case of Sector Specific Sticky Wages," *American Economic Review*, vol. 66 (1976): 502–508. These issues are taken up for discussion in Chapter 9.

16. See V. S. Vyas and George Mathai, "Farm and Non-Farm Employment in Rural Areas—A Perspective for Planning," *Economic and Political Weekly*, vol. 13 (Feb. 1978): 333–347.

17. See V. S. Vyas, "Agriculture: The Next Decade," *Technological Forecasting Social Change,* vol. 17 (1980): 259–269. Vyas also found in a recent study of five South Asian countries that there have been steady increases in marginal and small farm households over the last three decades. Unless economic viability of their holdings can be ensured, the temptation to migrate to acquire social assets in the urban informal sector will remain.
18. See Bhalla and Chadha, "Green Revolution and the Small Peasant."

8

Corruption Systems
in Developing Countries

The analysis so far has been confined to describing the positive role social assets play in creating earning opportunities for the poor, but the same informal contracting processes can be equally well utilized by officials within public organizations to appropriate earning opportunities.

The chapter utilizes the framework developed so far to explain the nature and scope of corruption systems in developing countries. Informal behavioral contracts can enable officials to acquire earning capabilities, to which they are not legally entitled, within public organizations. In extreme cases, unorganized or illegal markets can develop for public offices, transfers, and postings.[1] An examination of these issues is necessary for one to appreciate how socially inefficient informal institutions can vitiate the implementation of developmental programs.

The analysis will cover the issue of corruption in public agencies in general, using Robert Wade's case study on irrigation systems in India whenever necessary for purposes of illustration.[2] The term *public official* is used in a general sense to include any executive, legislative, or judicial employee of a government.

Three propositions are discussed and elaborated below. These are:

1. Corruption in developing countries consists of systematic exploitation of illegal income-earning opportunities within different administrative and delivery systems.
2. The enduring nature of these earning opportunities implies the creation of intangible property rights within the system. "Pur-

chases" of postings by officials are methods of acquiring access to these property rights.

3. These informal contracting processes outline the contours of recipient systems that often vitiate universal access to the benefits of developmental programs.

Each of these propositions is taken up for discussion in the next section.

Earning Opportunities in Public Services

The earning opportunities in public agencies can be considered to arise from two sources. First, in the *traditional* functions of administration, existing institutions serve relatively large populations. As a result, the services offered by these institutions are constantly facing excess demand despite being designed to offer universal and free public services. Second, in *developmental* functions of administration, institutions created to promote economic development such as those providing urban and rural delivery systems and those granting socially valued but scarce resources, also face excess demand. This is because buyers perceive marginal net benefits in acquiring the goods and services delivered by them.[3]

In both these situations, high private valuations are attached to these institutions, automatically endowing them with rent-generating capabilities. Officials who control access to such scarce economic goods therefore have several rent-seeking (more accurately rent-sharing) opportunities. Unlike Krueger's analysis of rent seeking, which looks at rent generated by a specific government policy, these rent-seeking opportunities are almost univeral in public institutions.

A second and even more serious form of earning opportunities in a developing country arises when officials within delivery systems and regulatory bodies are able to exploit information asymmetries in the system to defraud the exchequer.

Rent-Seeking Opportunities

Rent-seeking and defrauding opportunities are examined separately for public officials employed in both the traditional and the developmental functions of the government.

In the traditional functions of public administration: Among the traditional functions of public administration, rent-seeking opportunities arise because of inefficient enforcement of property rights and regulations.

Take, for instance, a medium farmer's property rights on something as basic and as tangible as land. Inefficiencies in the legal and administrative system impose costs to this person for simply enforcing his recognized property rights, as discussed in Chapter 2. If someone were to encroach on his land, legal redress through the civil and criminal courts is expensive both in terms of time and lawyers' fees. If he wishes to sell the land, getting the deed registered in the local subregistry office again may involve a long wait. Even securing help from the police to simply enforce his rights when his house is burglarized is an arduous task. Many such illustrations can be given, such as difficulties in obtaining (a) the renewal of a motor vehicle license, (b) a gun license, or (c) even a simple certificate of residence.

The reason for these difficulties in enforcing one's rights is the relative scarcity of administrative agencies. These agencies in developing countries are responsible for very large or dispersed populations, so the grievances of many law-abiding citizens will remain unattended unless they are able to beat the system by either social connections or bribes. Where, in addition, time has high opportunity costs, bribes become an easy way of jumping the queue. Rashid has given a fascinating account of how telephone operators in India arrange for international calls on priority basis after receiving regular payoffs.[4]

These bribes can therefore be regarded as earnings arising out of exploiting rent-seeking opportunities. They lead to market-clearing responses for inefficiencies from what economic theory ostensibly regard as free public goods.

In the developmental functions of public administration: Unlike the traditional functions, where rent-seeking opportunities arise because of private costs in utilizing public institutions, in developmental functions analogous opportunities arise because buyers perceive appropriable benefits from the services offered by public agencies. These services (a) deliver newly created common property rights such as irrigation water, public highways, health services, and rural electrification, and (b) control access to vital economic goods such as seeds, fertilizer, and import licenses. In all these situations, if buyers can increase their allocations from the administrative system, they can increase their private wealth. A farmer upstream in the distributary system of irrigation canals is, for instance, aware of the marginal net benefits that can be obtained by him if he were able to divert a larger allocation from the common property right of irrigation water. In these situations, informal markets are created by which these services receive valuations much higher than the rates charged by official policy.

In both the traditional and developmental functions, public officials are thus able to function as discriminating monopolists and fix market-clearing rates for the services being offered. These earnings are in the nature of rents earned by their control of access to scarce services. In some very traditional departments like the subregistry office referred to earlier, such rents are so highly institutionalized that earning opportunities are not reduced when a person is transferred from one posting to another. He can simply slip into a new post and begin collecting his bribes or rents.[5]

Defrauding Opportunities

The second form of earning opportunities involves systematic defrauding operations. These arise (a) when public agencies are not clearly accountable or (b) when public opinion simply does not exist as a countervailing force. One can hypothesize that opportunities for defrauding exist to a much larger degree in the developmental functions of public agencies when compared to the traditional functions.

In development projects, whether it be irrigation, public health, or rural electrification programs, large allocations of funds are awarded from the national or provincial governments to rural areas. In these essentially state-focused programs, the intended beneficiaries are to varying degrees unaware of the exact composition of expenditures. In any case, information on projects is highly asymmetric because of the technical complexities of the work.

Systematic defrauding opportunities arise during (a) implementation of construction programs and (b) maintenance of public delivery systems. For instance, suppose tenders are called for a highway construction project worth $1 million. Tender papers and award of contract to the lowest bidder will be perfectly in order. Informal agreements (before or after the contract finalization) will, however, be reached by which the contractor is allowed to use substandard material and pad up labor costs so that his costs amount to only $750,000. The balance $250,000 is then shared between the concerned individuals. Public officials in these situations have to devise elaborate mechanisms by which the informal agreements are properly honored. These issues will be taken up for analysis in the next section.

In the traditional functions of public administration, the opportunities for defrauding the system are considerably less. The reasons for this are several. First, many of these functions are finalized and implemented at a local level, and are relatively simple to comprehend. For instance, if funds are allocated to reexcavate an irrigation tank in a village, local inhabitants are aware of the nature of the work. However, when rural power relations are unequal, systematic defrauding through informal arrangement between officials and some influential villagers can take place. Obviously, the scope of such arrangements will depend on the vitality of village institutions. In some traditional functions like the subregistry office, while rent-seeking opportunities exist, there is no scope for defrauding opportunities because of the nature of the public function.

Predictably, the only department with comparable scope for defrauding opportunities is the police force, especially in urban and semiurban areas. A common phenomenon experienced by administrators working in rural India is that most subinspectors of police know much more of crime in their jurisdiction than they reveal officially.

Property Rights Aspects of Informal Contracting Arrangements

The last section has revealed that earning opportunities arise because of either rent-seeking or defrauding arrangements. These opportunities have become˜ so institutionalized that, as Wade has commented, kickback rates actually get quoted in many public agencies. One can reasonably hypothesize that officials in developing countries can, if they want to, secure access to enduring earning opportunities. In the rent-seeking category, the earning opportunities are given, but can marginally be increased or decreased over time. In defrauding opportunities, earnings depend on more systematic organization because agreements and promises actually have to be enforced. In both cases, clearly, officials have access to a set of intangible property rights akin to the concept of goodwill discussed earlier.

In both situations, the formal system of contracts has been institutionalized into the defrauding mechanism.[6] After the acceptance of tenders, the officials and contractors have to work out a mechanism by which bargains are maintained. One can generalize that three options are available for enforcing these contracts. These are:

1. Officials may become part owners or creditors of contracting firms (more like interlocked directorates). Contracts become internalized between the contract-awarding authority and the

contractor. But as an administrative system is hierarchical, arrangements still have to be made to ensure that other staff members do not interfere with the execution of these contracts.

2. Hierarchical chains of command may be utilized to enforce contracts. Such networks become important because tenders (especially for large contracts) are accepted at one (superior) level, and implemented at another (subordinate) level.

3. Parochial networks such as kinship groups, castes or tribes could be another form by which these arrangements are fully internalized.

The Importance of Transfers

Transfers of officials in these situations acquire two dimensions. First, jobs where intangible property rights through defrauding opportunities exist can be expected to have high valuations attached to them. For such jobs, markets can easily develop among corrupt officials. Second, postings are also sought after for access to material comforts, such as convenient housing, schools, social life, and easy communications with metropolitan centers. This factor assumes great importance in developing countries because many postings with high earning opportunities may also involve undergoing considerable personal and domestic hardship.

One cannot determine which of these two factors dominates an individual's calculations. Given a choice between large earnings opportunities through defrauding in remote parts of a country, and a lower earning capability, plus a more comfortable existence in a large town, many may prefer the latter. Of course, a pure income maximizer would prefer the former option!

In these markets, transfers—or simply threats of transfers—serve a dual purpose when defrauding opportunities are present. First, individuals pay for postings and transfers to secure access to existing informal property rights at particular locations. One could consider these "purchases" analogous to a business firm's purchasing goodwill associated with a brand name. Second, and of equal importance, threats of transfers are methods of exercising hierarchical discipline for maintaining the value of property rights created out of defrauding opportunities, so that informal contracts worked out at a superior level are faithfully executed by subordinates.

Interestingly, contracts through parochial networks utilizing established conventions and norms such as caste, tribal loyalties, and kinship ties will exhibit features very similar to the peanut seller model discussed in Chapter 5. Such enforcement mechanisms are clearly easier to administer than a transfer-based system. One can hypothesize that with growing heterogeneity of the work force, parochial considerations will automatically give way to more impersonal contracting mechanisms. Corruption systems, however, continue to retain their income-earning capabilities.

Implications

The analysis indicates that, owing to informational asymmetries between the principals and agents, unorganized markets develop within public organizations that vitiate development effort. There is a need for social scientists to recognize the significance of these informal institutions as informal recipient systems of development programs. Particularly in backward rural regions, delivery systems have to be made to deliver their goods and services to the intended beneficiaries, and not to these endogenous recipient systems that have succeeded in systematizing corruption. The implications of these systems are discussed next.

The prevalence of rent-seeking opportunities is an issue that has been common to most countries facing constant shortages during the process of economic growth. As was discussed earlier, it is a market response that is likely to persist until economic growth reduces the need for seeking out such rents. These opportunities, in fact, end up allocating services and resources to those individuals who are able to secure the highest marginal net benefits, and so have been generally ignored by economists.

The efficiency aspect of rent-seeking opportunities is easily negated by two sets of factors. First, in practice, the dividing line between rent-seeking and defrauding opportunities is a very thin one. Rashid has shown, for instance, in his telephone case study, how the telephone operators increased their income earnings through false billings. Second, the equity implications are highly adverse. Apart from reallocating valuable and scarce goods and services away from the poor to the affluent, such systems create large reserves of "black money" that is used unproductively for overvaluing urban property, purchase of gold and jewelry, and gets used for other forms of conspicuous consumption. Not surprisingly, the entire political and administrative system operates, to use Lakshmi Jain's expression, as "grass without roots."[7]

The added dimension of defrauding opportunities compounds this problem. A large percentage of funds is siphoned off through informal institutions to unintended recipients. The actual recipients often end up with far less than they were ostensibly to receive. Irrigation channels silt up, soil conservation programs lead to more erosion, highways are dotted with potholes, buildings have large leaky patches and peeling walls. The list can be an endless one, with smugglers attaining social respectability, adultered food sold with impunity, and criminal syndicates operating in open defiance of the law.

Suggested Solutions

The question that arises, then, is how is one to tackle this problems? There is no doubt that corruption systems are ultimately a function of the level of economic opportunities and literacy. But even with low literacy levels, the problem can be tackled by mobilizing public opinion and strengthening grass roots institutions. Villages even today do administer some of their existing common property rights through group cooperation. With organizational interventions they could be made to monitor corruption in delivery systems.

Taking rent-seeking opportunities first, an effective method is for the government or village groups themselves to take over the role of discriminating monopolists—for instance, in routine adminstrative matters like renewal of car licenses or issue of cement permits. The government could alter the rules so that applicants who want to jump the queue can do so by paying a premium to the state rather than to an official. In the delivery of inputs like water or fertilizers, informal village groups could be allowed to charge premiums above a base rate, and collectively appropriate the surpluses for developing their common properties such as schools, playgrounds, and cultural centers.

For defrauding opportunities, strong public policies are needed on many fronts.[8] First, whenever technical work is undertaken there has to be independent technical audit. Usually, investigation of technically complex projects is perfunctory and undertaken by persons from the department. Unless this system is changed to audits by competent, independent evaluators, it will be impossible to actually gauge the extent to which defrauding takes place.

Second, greater awareness has to be inculcated among potential beneficiaries of developmental programs about the programs. Corruption of the defrauding variety is a function of two factors:

1. Asymmetry of information between public officials delivering goods and services and beneficiaries of the program. If the latter are aware of programs and schemes, automatic counter-

vailing power is established. Constant dissemination of information about the nature of developmental programs is necessary among all the intended beneficiaries. Obviously, strong local institutions of self-government and rising literacy will contribute to reducing informational imbalance.

2. Level of economic and social development of the region. The easiest areas to defraud are the poorest regions of a country. Poverty and illiteracy are usually closely associated, and people in these areas are simply unaware of the value of their rights to newly created common properties. In these regions, parochial considerations based on caste or kinship loyalties can effortlessly divert public funds. Whenever developmental programs are implemented in very poor areas, organizational intervention is essential for developing the desired recipient systems.

Finally, the law has to recognize that defrauding the state by willfully appropriating newly created common property rights is a criminal offense of the same magnitude as extortion. There is a need to recognize that economic crimes are as serious as crimes against private property and fellow human beings. The total amorality of the system today in developing countries is also due to a long-standing perception of corruption as rent seeking.

Conclusion

This chapter has demonstrated that intangible property rights are created and protected in illegal markets in a manner similar to those discussed in the previous chapters. There is a need for economists and other social scientists to pay more attention to this great black hole of development economics and public policy. In the final chapter, these ideas are integrated with the analysis of previous chapters to assess the problems and policies in developing countries today.

Notes and References

1. This chapter is based on an article by N. Vijay Jagannathan, "Corruption, Property Rights and Delivery Systems," which has appeared in *World Development*, vol. 14, no. 1 (1986): 127–132.
2. R. Wade, "The Market for Public Office: Why the Indian State Is Not Better at Development," *World Development*, vol. 13, no. 4 (1985), provides some evidence of the ideas discussed in this chapter.

3. I have deliberately not used the words *regulatory* and *developmental* as functions of administration because in many regulatory functions, such as administering the flow of water into an irrigation distributary or granting a cement permit, the function is developmental as well. The terms *traditional* and *developmental* are used instead.

4. Of course, some enterprising officials do try to alter the patterns of price discrimination, especially when a region is experiencing rapid economic growth, and buyers are willing to pay higher bribes.

5. Wade has discussed these issues at length in his articles (note 2).

6. See Salim Rashid, "Public Utilities in Egalitarian LDCs," *Kyklos*, vol. 34, fasc. 3 (1981): 448–460.

7. See Lakshmi C. Jain, "Grass Without Roots: Rural Development Under Government Auspicies," *Mainstream* (Oct. 1982).

8. In a technical scheme, simply transferring the department from state focus to district focus may not make any appreciable difference because no one will be able to assess the nature of fraud taking place during highly technical operations.

9

Policy Interventions
in a Rent-Seeking Society

The study so far explained the manner in which behavioral relations are utilized productively in unorganized markets. Through informal contracts, the poor as well as the affluent are able to capture rent-seeking opportunities in both production and exchange. This final chapter discusses some implications of intangible property rights for developmental policy.

In the first section, the importance of intangible property rights is discussed and the nature of their changes during economic development is analyzed. The second section discusses past policy experience. The third section suggests some implications of these concepts for the design and implementation of public policies.

The Importance of Intangible Property Rights

Unorganized markets have so far remained fairly nebulous concepts in development economics. Although an awareness does exist of the importance of the "parallel economy" of tax evaders and criminals, there has been an inadequate appreciation of (a) the parallel economy of the poor and (b) the enduring nature of relations in all such markets. This study suggests that understanding the workings of all unorganized markets is essential for designing an effective policy to promote equitable development.

As a first step, the process of production and exchange in these markets should be explicitly recognized by social scientists. These processes cannot be understood by mechanically extending the paradigms based on neoclassical or Marxian traditions, because the for-

118

mal law does not define the parameters of economic activities in un-organized markets.[1]

In such markets, the absence of formal institutions and the high cost of information have led to near universality of rent-seeking opportunities. Through a system of implicit contracts, the poor as well as some of the rich are able to appropriate earnings steadily over time.

An economy can be visualized to have within it several overlapping subsystems, each affording its members access to varying amounts of economic rents as entitlements. At one end of the scale are subsystems of dishonest traders, corrupt officials, and leaders of crime syndicates, who take advantage of institutional weaknesses to appropriate sizable wealth. At the other end of the scale are the hapless destitute without any access to economic entitlements. In between are the millions of poor, whose levels of poverty are determined by differentials in access to legal and social assets. The members of the many existing subsystems can be described as belonging to different recipient systems.

The regular behavioral relations within these systems considerably blur the formation of classes as suggested by Marxian literature.[2] Power relations may be unequal and information may be asymmetric between the rich and the poor, but the latter have usually invested considerable time and energy in developing their social assets. Quite understandably, many of the poor have vital stakes in the economic system. It is only when drastic political or social upheavals destroy the opportunities for maintaining these contracts that a uniform class of the poor is created.[3]

Inequalities of access to earning opportunities are likely to be enduring over a period of time, but rapid economic growth, or changes in inflation rate can be expected to alter the structure of recipient systems.

Take growth in national income. At first one can expect the benefits to trickle down to existing recipient systems in an economy: Villagers could derive some benefits from the green revolution, street hawkers could increase the value of their social assets from urban growth, and subcontracting opportunities for small firms could increase, to name just a few. In the short run, informal groups can be expected to police their social assets zealously.

Rapid economic growth throws up numerous opportunities for earning livelihood, and as a result, existing social assets may no longer appear worthwhile. Menial jobs and marginal occupations gradually lose their attractiveness as earning opportunities. One can thus expect social assets to undergo qualitative changes. Social assets policed by traditional norms and conventions may be replaced by new economics-based conventions, as new rent-seeking opportunities evolve.

One cannot, however, predict that general multilateral relations will disappear. In some cases, the flexibility and structural strengths of informal groups can enable them to seize earning opportunities through subcontracting; large, highly motivated business enterprises of the "Theory Z" variety may evolve. Some of the large enterprises in Japan and South Korea had their origins as humble informal sector institutions.[4]

However, for growth impulses to trickle down to the very poor who have no social assets, the time span required may be long and uncertain. People having no entitlements in the system are caught in a poverty trap, from which an exit is possible only by policy interventions.[5]

Inflation and Social Assets

High inflation rates only add to the problems of the poor. Received theory has reached a consensus that increases in food prices affect the welfare of the poor, because such people are usually net buyers of food.[6]

This study has argued that apart from basic food, the poor also mortgage their property rights from developmental programs so that they are able to acquire purchasing power for consumer goods. Tobacco products, liquor, movies, and other consumer goods are sold with high-pressure advertising and catchy slogans. These commodities quickly become necessities, especially when they are addictive in nature.

When inflation rates increase, some traders and hawkers can be expected to benefit at the expense of a majority of the poor. Apart from creating artificial scarcities to increase prices further, adulteration of consumer goods and foodstuffs occurs.

Such defrauding opportunities arise for two reasons. First, for some of the more addictive consumer goods, the poor simply do not have the flexibility in their entitlements to match the price increases that take place during inflation. Second, because of intense poverty and ignorance, discount rates for the future are often very high, and the poor consume adulterated products despite the long-term damage to physical health and well-being.

One can conclude that high inflation rates increase the inequalities in unorganized markets. They also generate negative externalities in the health and well-being of the majority of the poor.

To sum up, as informally contracted recipient systems are endogenously created, one has to recognize that it is not easy for public policy to alter them. The real challenge of a policy maker is to devise methods by which the existing informal institutions can be made more socially useful. With this aim in mind, the next sections examine policy experience and future prospects.

Social Assets and Past Policies

The previous section has shown that (a) social assets create a social security net for a majority of the absolute poor and that (b) informal institutions structure a market's penalty-reward system. In these concluding sections, some institutional implications of social welfare policies in developing countries are examined so that guidelines can be framed for future policies.

Among developing countries there has been a fairly rich set of policy interventions designed to protect social entitlements. Two experiences sum up the policy alternatives that have been tried. The first, or the radical, approach has been to institutionalize rights arising out of social assets along with socializing most property rights. The second experience, which can be termed as the moderate approach, has sought to guarantee certain basic entitlements without making any major institutional changes in formal property rights.

The Radical Solution

The radical solution has been the Chinese or Cuban model, where the social usufructuary rights arising out of social assets have been institutionalized.[7] This experience has come the closest to legalizing all social assets by creating a social security net of state-guaranteed entitlements. Available evidence indicates that this approach does effectively succeed in eliminating some of the worst manifestations of poverty such as starvation and malnutrition.

The radical solution has undoubtedly been a successful defensive measure against absolute poverty. It has created state-sponsored social assets to replace informally contracted relations. One byproduct of such measures, however, is that they also simultaneously eliminate the wealth-generating and efficiency aspects of social assets. When entitlements are given to individuals by state fiat, rather than being supported by endogenous informal contracts, various wealth-generating externalities that accompany informal behavioral relations are also eliminated. The most important casualty, as the Chinese experience has indicated, is the loss of incentive to be efficient. Free-rider and shirking problems increase as in any organized sector institution, resulting in a growth of inefficiency, and mounting deadweight losses.[8]

The Moderate Approach

The moderate approach has been the experience of most developing countries. They have attempted variants of what can be termed as a basic needs strategy. A core of services in areas such as nutrition, health, sanitation, and housing have been provided without directly interfering with informal contracting processes.[9] While the state tries to provide some vital services, individuals remain free to develop social assets in unorganized markets. The experience of countries trying out the moderate approach has been mixed, but one common feature that has been observed is the limited success of programs. A few indicators such as literacy and nutritional levels have usually shown remarkable improvement, while other indicators have suggested relatively unsatisfactory performance.

This study explains the reasons for this observed feature. A Basic Needs strategy's success will depend on the nature of endogenous recipient systems. Even in the absence of corruption systems, widespread parallel contracting processes result in the poor's mortgaging their future property rights for current purchasing power. As a result, a program's efficacy depends on the extent to which targeted benefits are retained by the poor. Often, through informal contracts, the affluent are able to appropriate the benefits.[10]

Public policy can be hypothesized to create three types of property rights. These are:

1. Tangible and appropriable property rights on benefits that can be easily transferred. For instance, if a housing program is implemented for the landless, timber and cement may be appropriated by landowners. If a package of expensive inputs is given to marginal farmers, they very soon find their way to the farms of large landowners. Good quality clothing, sugar, kerosene— all similarly end up with affluent villagers.[11]

2. Tangible but inappropriable benefits. Some deliveries are not valued by affluent villagers, and so do not get appropriated. Cheap cloth, coarse grain, small livestock usually are not easily mortgaged. Social conventions and norms play an important role in determining which rights should not be appropriated. In ur-

ban areas, common facilities such as portable water and improved sanitation have a similar characteristic.

3. Intangible property rights that cannot be easily transferred. Most of these arise out of programs involving direct consumption by recipients of services. For example, a primary school's budgetary allocations depend on pupil enrollments. Similarly, a nutritional program such as midday meals for either children or expectant mothers depends on the physical presence of recipients. So it is not surprising to find that greatest success has been feasible for public policy in these areas.

A basic needs strategy very often ends up alleviating poverty in a manner quite unintended by the policy maker. Massive misappropriations of public welfare funds in rural areas takes place through two recipient systems. First, corruption systems within public organizations divert resources away from *all* intended beneficiaries. Second, resources get reallocated at the microeconomic level between the affluent and the poor through localized informal contracting arrangements.

Prospects

This study has indicated two features of unorganized markets of interest to public policy. First, the poor use informal contracts to create endogenous social security nets. Second, public organizations, when designed as delivery systems, may have within them organized corruption systems. When large sums of developmental funds are funneled through poorly paid officials, many of these officials are tempted to resort to their own set of informal contracts to capture earning opportunities.

In a radical strategy of the Chinese or Cuban model, while absolute poverty (of those with no entitlements) is eliminated, institutional efficiency of unorganized markets is drastically reduced. The moderate policy, in contrast, while retaining the wealth-generating aspects, has no effective social security nets for the poorest section of society; those who have been unable to secure rents. In both strategies there is the need for an organizational design that takes care of the twin goals of ensuring universal access to earning opportunities and reducing the scope of corruption systems.

How can this be done? There is obviously a need for developing the poor's countervailing power, through full-scale participation. An organizational design is vital—one through which the felt needs and grievances of the poor can be heard during the formulation and implementation of developmental programs. The essential preconditions in designing such programs are:

1. Local institutions of self-government have to be designed or revitalized, so that communities are given a forum to explain local issues and understand the direction and details of public policy.
2. Information on developmental programs should be available through the media. Radio, television, and billboards should disseminate the details of plans and programs intended for specific communities.

Once these preconditions are met, a pragmatic solution for alleviation of poverty is for the policy maker to identify and develop property rights of the poor on assets that are, at present, latent. For instance, even the poorest of the poor usually own a few chickens, pigs, and poultry. These assets do not have much mortgaging potential because of their low utility to affluent villagers. If a policy maker is able to identify suitable methods of upgrading their quality (modern technology offers numerous opportunities in this regard), and provide support for marketing these products, supplementary sources of income and employment can be created without altering existing informal institutional arrangements.[12]

A second area where a policy maker can hope to achieve results is in utilizing existing behavioral externalities within informal groups as an institutional resource of the Chinese clan variety in production. Chapter 3 described one example of how the bidi or country cigar industry was established using the structural strengths of informal institutions in production. Similar examples can be cited from traditional methods of irrigation, and from subcontracting in the urban informal sector. Behavioral relations among informal group members provide several possibilities for diffusing technology and promoting economic growth, particularly if the strategy retains these people in their rural residences.[13]

To sum up, policy could be directed toward two areas of research. First, technological and marketing studies should be conducted to identify and convert many of the latent assets of the poor into income-generating assets. While this policy does not disrupt existing informal contractual arrangements, in the long run it could provide the poor with sources of regenerative income. Second, the feasibility of organizational design for utilizing existing informal groups as an efficient clan variety of cooperative needs to be researched. The policy implications of this measure are likely to be several in both rural markets and urban informal sector markets of developing countries.

Conclusion

Poverty and inequality of income in the developing countries has been the focus of much debate and discussion over the last three decades. Many suggestions and solutions have been put forward, covering a whole spectrum of ideologies and beliefs. The preceding pages have attempted to show that human beings, unlike robots and machines, constantly strive for better prospects for themselves through complex contracting processes. To understand the dynamics of change, one has to appreciate the nature of informal contracts as social engineers, bridging organizational failures so that every section of the population gets an opportunity to participate in the growth process. This is perhaps the most basic of basic human needs—the need to give everyone not just a charitable gift of food, clothing, and shelter, but more important, access to economic growth.

"Man is born free, and everywhere he is in chains," commented Rousseau two centuries ago. It is hoped that this study has provided new insights into these chains so that we know which chains to strengthen and which to weaken for all the hungry and the wretched of human society.

Notes and References

1. Received theory should not therefore be applied mechanically to explain economic relationships in developing countries. As this study has demonstrated, simple principles of microeconomics can be utilized to explain the formation and use of social assets.
2. See Giddens, "Capitalism and Modern Social Theory"; Amin, "Imperialism and Unequal Development." In fact, informal institutions in developing countries may have nothing in common with institutions and organizations set up by formal law. This study suggests that the induced innovation hypothesis needs also to be reevaluated. See Vernon Ruttan and Hans Binswanger, *Induced Innovation: Technologies, Institutions and Development* (Baltimore: Johns Hopkins University Press, 1978).
3. Strong dictatorships that enforce the property rights of a few affluent people would lead to the destruction of many social assets of the poor.
4. Hitachi, for instance, began as a small unit in the informal sector. For

Theory Z see William G. Ouchi and Raymond Price, "Hierarchies, Clans and Theory Z: A New Perspective on Organizational Development," *Organizational Dynamics* (Autumn 1978): 25–44.

5. The worst forms of destitution can be found among the urban poor when individuals have no entitlements whatsoever.

6. See John W. Mellor and Gunvant M. Desai, *Agricultural Change and Rural Poverty* (Baltimore: Johns Hopkins University Press, 1985), for related discussion.

7. See "China's Changed Road to Development," Special Issue of *World Development*, vol. 11, no. 8 (Aug. 1983), particularly Introduction and article by A. Watson, "Agricultural Looks for the Shoes That Fit: The Production Responsibility System and its Implications," pp. 205–230.

8. For a useful discussion on the Chinese and Tanzanian incentives debate see Louis Putterman, "Extrinsic vs. Intrinsic Problems of Agricultural Cooperation Anti-Incentivism in Tanzania and China," Working Paper in Comparative Development (Brown University, 1983).

9. Of course, the Basic Human Needs strategy is specially associated with a specific program for human resource development. The term here is being loosely applied to any welfare-oriented developmental program. For a comprehensive discussion on Basic Needs see Paul P. Streeten, "Basic Needs: Some Unsettled Questions," *World Development*, vol. 12, no. 9 (Sept. 1984). Also see David Morawetz, *Twenty-five Years of Economic Development* (Baltimore: Johns Hopkins University Press, 1978).

10. See L. C. Jain, "Grass without Roots." Jain's thesis is that the failure of delivery systems has been because the administrative system consistently fails to deliver the goods. Our view is that this feature has been caused by prevalent informal contracting processes.

11. In urban areas, transferability takes a different form. Tangible property rights are likely to reach the beneficiaries, although they may use the benefits in a manner different from that intended by public policy. For instance, permanent housing allocated to slum dwellers may be sublet because of variations in individual preference functions.

12. Several examples of possibilities can be suggested. For instance, traditional varieties of goats can be cross-bred with exotic varieties to increase yield of milk and meat. Similar parallels can be suggested for poultry, pigs, and fisheries. Animal husbandry offers tremendous untapped prospects for developing latent assets. Marketing possibilities have increased greatly following the urban expansion and changes in dietary preferences to poultry, fish and meat products. The price of meat or animal based products has been consistently increasing as a result of these features.

13. See Cheung, "Contractual Nature of the Firm"; Landa, "Theory of Ethnically Homogeneous Middlemen Group"; Hariss, "Small Scale Production and Labour Markets"; and Watanabe, "Entrepreneurship in Small Enterprises," for related discussion. For another useful study in the Philippines on how informal groups of farmers utilized their behavioral relations to tackle labor shortages, see Gelia T. Castillo, "Has Bayanihan Gone Out of Style?" *Philippine Agriculture*, vol. 65, no. 4 (Oct.–Dec. 1982).

Bibliography

Accountants International Study Group. *Accounting for Goodwill: Current Practices in Canada, the United Kingdom and the United States.* New York, 1975.

Ackerlof, George. "Market for 'Lemons': Quality Uncertainty and the Market Mechanism." *Quarterly Journal of Economics* 84 (August 1970): 488–500.

Ackerman, Bruce A. *Economic Foundations of Property Law.* Little Brown & Co. (Canada), 1975.

Alchian, Armen A., and Harold B. Demsetz. "Production, Information Costs and Economic Organization." *American Economic Review* 62, no. 5 (December 1972): 777–795.

Amin, Samir. *Imperialism and Unequal Development.* New York: Monthly Review Press, 1977.

Bamisaiye, Anne. "Begging in Ibadan, Southern Nigeria." *Human Organization* 33, no. 2 (Summer 1974): 197–202.

Banerjee, Biswajit. "The Role of the Informal Sector in the Migration Process: A Test of Probabilistic Migration Models and Labour Market Segmentation for India." *Oxford Economic Papers* 35 (1983): 399–422.

Banerjee, Biswajit. "Social Networks in the Migration Process: Empirical Evidence on Chain Migration in India." *Journal of Developing Areas* 17 (1983): 185–196.

Bardhan, P. "Wages and Unemployment in a Poor Agrarian Economy: A Theoretical and Empirical Analysis." *Journal of Political Economy* 87, no. 3 (1978): 497–500.

Bardhan, P., and Ashok Rudra. "Terms and Conditions of Labor Contracts in Agriculture: Results of a Survey in West Bengal in 1979." *Oxford Bulletin of Economics and Statistics* 43, no. 1 (February 1983): 89–111.

Bardhan, P., and Ashok Rudra. "Interlocking Factor Markets and Agrarian Development: A Review of Issues." *Oxford Economic Papers* 32 (1980): 82–90.

Barzel, Yoram. "Fallacies of Information Costs." *Journal of Law and Economics* 31 (September 1978).

Basu, Kaushik. "Implicit Interest Rate, Usury and Isolation in Backward Agriculture." *Cambridge Journal of Economics* 8, no. 2 (June 1984): 145–160.

Ben Porath, Yoram. "The F-Connection: Families, Friends and Firms, and Organizations of Exchange." *Population and Development Review* 6, no. 1 (1980): 1–31.

127

Berry, Sara. "The Food Crisis and Agrarian Change in Africa: A Review Essay." *African Studies Review* 27, no. 2 (June 1984): 59–112.

Beteille, Andre. *Inequality among Men.* Oxford: Basil Blackwell, 1977.

Bhaduri, Amit. "On Formation of Usurious Interest Rates in Backward Agriculture." *Cambridge Journal of Economics* 1 (1977): 341–352.

Bhagwati, Jagdish N., and T. N. Srinivasan. "On Re-analysing the Harris Todaro Model: Policy Rankings in the Case of Sector-Specific Sticky Wages." *American Economic Review* 64 (1976): 502-508.

Bhalla, G. S., and G. K. Chadha. *Green Revolution and the Small Peasant.* New Delhi: Concept Publishing Co., 1983.

Bhalla, Sheila. "New Relations of Production in Haryana Agriculture." *Economic and Political Weekly* (March 1976).

Biggs, Stephen D., and Edward J. Clay. *Generation and Diffusion of Agricultural Technology: A Review of Theories and Experience.* Geneva: International Labour Office, 1983.

Binswanger, Hans P., and Mark R. Rosenzweig. "Behavioral and Material Determinants of Production Relations in Agriculture." Discussion paper ARU 5, Research Unit, Agriculture and Rural Development Department, World Bank (June 1982).

Blaug, Mark. "Human Capital Investment: A Slightly Jaundiced Survey." *Journal of Economic Literature* 14, no. 3 (September 1976): 827–855.

Blyn, George. "The Green Revolution Revisited." *Economic Development and Cultural Change* 31, no. 4 (July 1983): 705–726.

Buchanan, James, with R. Tollison and Gordon Tullock. *Towards a Theory of Rent Seeking Society.* Texas A&M Press, 1980.

Burt, Robert S. *Toward a Structural Theory of Action.* New York: Academic Press, 1982.

Chenery, Hollis, with Ahluwalia, Bell, Duloy, and Jolly. *Redistribution with Growth.* World Bank, 1973.

Cheung, Steven N. S. "The Contractual Nature of the Firm." *Journal of Law and Economics* 26, no. 1 (April 1983): 1–23.

Clegg, Stewart, and David Dunkerly. *Organization, Class and Control.* London: Routledge Kegan & Paul, 1980.

Coase, Ronald. "The Problem of Social Cost." *Journal of Law and Economics* 13 (October 1960): 1–44.

Connell, John, and Michael Lipton. *Assessing Village Labor Situations.* New York: Oxford University Press, 1977.

Comanor, William S., and Thomas A. Wilson. *Advertising and Market Power.* Cambridge: Harvard University Press, 1974.

Coward, Walter, Jr. "Principles of Social Organization in an Indigenous Irrigation System." *Human Organization* 38, no. 1 (Spring 1978): 28–36.

Dalton, George, ed. *Research in Economic Anthropology,* vol. 4. New York: Jai Press, 1981.

Dalton, George, ed. *Tribal and Peasant Societies.* Austin: University of Texas Press, 1967.

Dandekar, V. M., and N. Rath. "Poverty in India." *Economic and Political Weekly* 6, nos. 1 & 2 (January 2, 9, 1971).

Dasgupta, Biplab. "Calcutta's Informal Sector." *Bulletin* 5, Institute of Development Studies, Sussex, 1973.

Dasgupta, Biplab, with Roy Laishley, Henry Lucas, and Brian Mitchell. *Village Society and Labor Use*. New York: Oxford University Press, 1977.

De Alessi, Louis. "Property Rights, Transactions Costs and X-efficiency." *American Economic Review* 73, no. 1 (March 1983): 64–81.

Dean, Robert D., with William H. Leahy and David L. McKee. *Spatial Economic Theory*. New York: Free Press, 1970.

Desai, B. M., and B. L. Tripathi. "Group Based Savings and Credit Programmes in Rural India." Paper presented at the ILO Workshop on Group Based Savings and Credit Programmes, Bogra, October 1983.

De Souza, Alfred. *The Indian City*. New Delhi: South Asia Books, 1977.

Doeringer, Peter B., and Michael J. Piore. *Internal Labor Markets and Manpower Analysis*. Lexington: D.C. Heath 1971.

Eswaran, Mukesh, and Ashok Kotwal. "A Theory of Two-Tier Labor Markets in Agrarian Economies." *American Economic Review* 75, no. 1 (1985): 162–177.

Frazier, Steve. "A Slum Black Market in Mexico City Is a Part of the Establishment." *Wall Street Journal* (March 25 1985).

Furubotn, Eirik G., and Svetozar Pejovich. *The Economics of Property Rights*. Cambridge: Ballinger Publishing Co., 1974.

Furubotn, Eirik G., and Svetozar Pejovich. "Property Rights and Economic Theory: A Survey of Recent Literature." *Journal of Economic Literature* 10 (1972): 1137–1178.

Geertz, Clifford. "The Bazaar Economy: Information and Change in Peasant Marketing." *American Economic Review* 68, no. 2 (May 1978): 28–31.

Giddens, Anthony. *Capitalism and Modern Social Theory, an Analysis of the Writings of Marx, Durkheim and Max Weber*. Cambridge: Cambridge University Press, 1971.

Goodell, Grace E. "Bugs, Bunds, Banks and Bottlenecks: Organizational Contradictions in the New Rice Technology." *Economic Development and Cultural Change* 33, no. 1 (October 1984).

Griffin, Keith. "Growth and Impoverishment in Rural Areas of Asia." *World Development* 7, nos. 4/5 (April/May 1979): 361–384.

Griffin, Keith, and A. R. Khan. "Poverty in the Third World. Ugly Facts and Fancy Models." *World Development* 6, no. 3 (March 1978): 295–304.

Guttman, Joel M. "Villages as Interest Groups: Demand for Agricultural Extension Services in India." *Kyklos* 33, fasc. 1 (1980): 122–141.

Hackenburg, Robert. "New Patterns of Urbanization in Southeast Asia." *Population and Development Review* 6, no. 3 (1980).

Hariss, John. "Small Scale Production and Labour Markets." *Economic and Political Weekly* 17, nos. 23 and 24 (1982).

Harris, John R., and Michael P. Todaro. "Migration, Unemployment and Development: A Two-sector Analysis." *American Economic Review* 60 (1971): 126–142.

Hayami, Yujiro, and Masao Kikuchi. *Asian Village Economy at the Crossroads*. Baltimore: University of Tokyo Press and Johns Hopkins University Press, 1982.

Herring, Ronald J., and Rex J. Edwards. "Guaranteeing Employment for the Rural Poor: Social Functions and Class Interests in the Employment Guarantee Scheme in Western India." *World Development* 11, no. 7 (1983): 575–592.

Hill, Polly. *Migrant Cocoa Farmers of Southern Ghana*. Cambridge: Cambridge University Press, 1970.

House, William J. "Nairobi's Informal Sector: Dynamic Entrepreneurs or Surplus Labor?" *Economic Development and Cultural Change* 32, no. 2 (January 1984): 277–302.

Hughes, Hugh P. *Goodwill in Accounting: A History of the Issues and Problems.* Georgia State University Press, 1982.

Jagannathan, N. Vijay. *The Bidi Industry of Murshidabad District.* Department of Labour, Government of West Bengal, Calcutta, 1974.

Jagannathan, N. Vijay, "Corruption, Property Rights and Delivery Systems." *World Development* 14, no. 1 (1986): 127–132.

Jagannathan, N. Vijay. "The Effects of Farakka Barrage on Jangipur Subdivision" (mimeo), 1974.

Jagannathan, N. Vijay. "Effects of Urbanization on Durgapur's Hinterland" (mimeo), 1976.

Jagannathan, N. Vijay. "The Jangal Mahals: A Socio-economic Survey" (mimeo), 1975.

Jain, L. C. "Grass without Roots: Rural Development under Government Auspices." *Mainstream* (October 1984).

Jodha, N. S. "Population Growth and the Decline of Common Property Rights." *Population and Development Review* 11, no. 2 (June 1985): 247–264.

Joshi, Vijay H. "Rural-Urban Migration, Urban Unemployment and Economic Development." Lecture at the Center for International Studies, Harvard University, April 24, 1981.

Joshi, Vijay H., and Heather Joshi. *Surplus Labour and the City: A Study of Bombay.* New York: Oxford University Press (1976).

Kang, Gay E., and Tai S. Kang. "The Korean Urban Shoeshine Gang: A Minority Community." *Urban Anthropology* 7, no. 2 (Summer 1978): 171–184.

Kidder, Robert. *Connecting Law and Society.* Englewood Cliffs, Prentice-Hall, 1983.

Klein B., R. G. Crawford, and A. Alchian. "Vertical Integration, Appropriable Rents, and the Competitive Contracting Process." *Journal of Law and Economics* 31, no. 2 (1978): 297–326.

Kosinsky, Leszek A., and Mansell R. Prothero. *People on the Move.* London: Methuen & Co., 1972.

Kothari, K. L. *Tribal Social Change in India.* Udaipur: Himanshu Publications, 1985.

Kravis, Irving B., with Alan Heston, Robert Summers, and Alicia Civitello. *International Comparison of Real Product and Purchasing Power.* Baltimore: Johns Hopkins University Press, 1978.

Krueger, Anne. "The Political Economy of a Rent Seeking Society." *American Economic Review* 64 (June 1974): 291–303.

Kurtz, Donald V. "Rotating Credit Association: An Adaptation to Poverty." *Human Organization* 32 (Spring 1973): 49–57.

Landa, Janet T. "Theory of Ethnically Homogeneous Middleman Group-Institutional Alternative to Contract Law." *Journal of Legal Studies* 10 (1981).

Leaf, Murray J. "The Green Revolution and Cultural Change in a Punjab Village 1965–1978." *Economic Development and Cultural Change* 2 (January 1983): 227–270.

Lewis, Arthur W. "Economic Development with Unlimited Supply of Labor." *Manchester School of Economics and Social Studies* (May 1954): 329–402.

Liebenstein, Harvey. "A Branch of Economics Is Missing, Micro-macro Theory." *Journal of Economic Literature* 17 (June 1979): 477–502.

Liebenstein, Harvey. "On the Economics of Conventions and Institutions: An Exploratory Survey." *Journal of Institutional and Theoretical Economics* 140 (1980): 74–86.

Liebenstein, Harvey. "X-efficiency: From Concept to Theory." *Challenge* 22 (September/October 1979): 13–22.

Lynch, Owen M. "Potters, Plotters, Prodders in a Bombay Slum: Marx and Meaning or Meaning vs. Marx." *Urban Anthropology* 8, no. 1 (Spring 1979): 1–28.

McGee, Terence G. "Peasants in Cities: A Paradox, a Paradox, a Most Ingenious Paradox." *Human Organization* 32, no. 2 (1973): 135–142.

Macneill, Ian R. "The Many Futures of Contracts." *Southern California Law Review* 47, no. 3 (May 1974): 691–816.

Maine, Sir Henry Sumner. *Ancient Law: Its Connection with Early History of Society, and Its Relations to Modern Ideas.* London: J. Murray & Co., 1861.

Mandelbaum, W. *Society in India: Organization and Continuity.* University of California Press, 1970.

Mazumdar, Dipak. "Segmented Labor Markets in LDCs." *American Economic Review* 73, no. 2 (May 1983): 254–259.

Mazumdar, Dipak. "The Urban Informal Sector." *World Development* 4, no. 8 (August 1976): 655–679.

Mellor, John W., and Gunvant M. Desai. *Agricultural Change and Rural Poverty.* Baltimore: Johns Hopkins University Press, 1985.

Mellor, John W., and Bruce F. Johnston. "World Food Equation." *Journal of Economic Literature* 22, no. 2 (June 1984): 531–574.

Mendelsohn, Oliver. "Pathology of the Indian Legal System." *Modern Asian Studies* 15 (1981): 823–864.

Mitra, Asok. "Calcutta's Backyard-1, Health and Wealth from Garbage." *The Statesman.* Calcutta, January 24, 1984.

Morawetz, David. *Twenty-five Years of Economic Development.* Baltimore: Johns Hopkins University Press, 1977.

Olson, Mancur. *Logic of Collective Action.* Cambridge: Harvard University Press, 1971.

Opp, Karl Dieter. "The Emergence and Effects of Social Norms: A Confluence of Some Hypotheses of Sociology and Economics." *Kyklos* 32, fasc. 4 (1979): 775–801.

Ouchi, William G., and Raymond Price. "Hierarchies, Clans and Theory Z: A New Perspective on Organizational Development." *Organizational Dynamics* (Autumn 1978): 25–44.

Papanek, Gustav F. "Real Wages, Growth, Inflation, Income Distribution and Politics in Pakistan, India, Bangladesh and Indonesia." Boston University Discussion Paper no. 27, Boston University (1979).

Papanek, Gustav F., and D. Kontjorojakti. "The Poor of Jakarta." *Economic Development and Cultural Change* 24, no. 1 (October 1975).

Pollak, Robert, A. "A Transactions Cost Approach to Families and Households." *Journal of Economic Literature* 23, no. 2 (June 1985): 581–608.

Porath, Yoram Ben. "F Connection: Families, Friends and Organization of Exchange." *Population and Development Review* 6, no. 1 (March 1980): 1–31.

Posner, Richard. *Economic Analysis of Law.* Boston: Little, Brown & Co, 1980.

Posner, Richard. "A Theory of Primitive Society with Special Reference to Law." *Journal of Law and Economics* 33, no. 1 (April 1980).

Putterman, Louis. "Extrinsic vs. Intrinsic Problems in Agricultural Cooperation, Anti-incentivism in Tanzania and China." Working Paper in Comparative Development, Brown University, 1983.

Quibria, M. "The Puzzle of Sharecropping: A Survey of Recent Evidence." *World Development* 12, no. 2 (February 1984): 103–114.

Ranis, Gustav, and J. C. H. Fei. "A Theory of Economic Development." *American Economic Review* 51, no. 4 (September 1961): 531–565.

Rashid, Salim. "Public Utilities in Egalitarian L.D.C.s." *Kyklos* 134, fasc. 3 (1981): 448–460.

Rosen, Sherwin. "Implicit Contracts: A Survey." *Journal of Economic Literature* 23, no. 3: 1144–1175.

Rudra, Ashok. *Indian Agricultural Economics: Some Myths and Realities.* New Delhi: Allied Publishers, 1982.

Ruttan, Vernon, and Hans P. Binswanger. *Induced Innovation: Technologies, Institutions and Development.* Baltimore: Johns Hopkins University Press, 1978.

Sabot, Richard H., ed. *Migration and the Labor Market in Developing Countries.* Boulder: Westview Press, 1982.

Schotter, Andrew. *An Economic Theory of Institutions.* New York: Cambridge University Press, 1980.

Sen, A. K. *Poverty and Famine: An Essay on Entitlement and Deprivation.* New York: Oxford University Press, 1981.

Sen, A. K. "Poverty and Unemployment in India: An Analysis of Recent Evidence." World Bank Staff Working Paper No. 417 (1980).

Sethuraman, S. V. *The Urban Informal Sector in Developing Countries.* Geneva: International Labour Office, 1981.

Simon, A., ed. *Research in Economic Anthropology*, vol. 4. New York: Jai Press, 1984.

Steiner, Peter O. "Markets." *International Encyclopaedia of Social Sciences* 9 (1968): 578–581.

Streeten, Paul P. "Basic Needs: Some Unsettled Questions." *World Development* 12, no. 9 (September 1984).

Stuyvesant, Peter. *The Ghetto Marketplace.* New York: Free Press, 1969.

Tollison, Robert D. "Rent Seeking: A Survey." *Kyklos* 35, fasc. 4 (1982): 575–602.

Umbeck, John. *A Theory of Property Rights.* Iowa State University Press, 1981.

Veblen, Thorstein. "On the Nature of Capital, Intangible Assets and the Pecuniary Magnate. *Quarterly Journal of Economics* 22 (1908): 104–136.

Vyas, V. S. "Agriculture: The Next Decade." *Technological Forecasting Social Change* 17 (1980): 259–269.

Vyas, V. S., and George Mathai. "Farm and Non-farm Employment in Rural Areas— A Perspective for Planning." *Economic and Political Weekly* 13 (February 1978): 333–347.

Wade, R. "Irrigation Reform in Conditions of Populist Anarchy: An Indian Case." *Journal of Developmental Studies* 14, no. 3 (1984).

Wade, R. "The Market for Public Office: Why the Indian State Is Not Better at Development." *World Development* 13, no. 4 (1985).

Wade, R. "The System of Administrative and Political Corruption: Canal Irrigation in South India." *Journal of Development Studies* 18, no. 3 (1984): 287–328.

Watanabe, S. "Entrepreneurship in Small Enterprises in Japanese Manufacturing." *International Labour Review* 104 (1971): 51–76.

Watson, A. "Agriculture Looks for the Shoes That Fit: The Production Responsibility System and Its Implications." *World Development* 11, no. 8 (August 1983): 205–230.

Weiszacker, Carl C. von. *Barriers to Entry*. Berlin: Springer Verlager, 1980.

Williamson, Oliver E. *Markets and Hierarchies. Analysis and Anti-trust Implications: A Study in the Economics of Internal Organization*. New York: Free Press, 1975.

Williamson, Oliver E. "Transactions Cost Economics; the Governance of Contractual Relations." *Journal of Law and Economics* 23, no. 2 (October 1979).

Zerbe, Richard O. *Research in Law and Economics*, vol. 2. Greenwich: Jai Press, 1980.

Index